PRESIDENTS
AS CANDIDATES

POLITICS AND POLICY IN AMERICAN INSTITUTIONS
VOLUME I
GARLAND REFERENCE LIBRARY OF SOCIAL SCIENCE
VOLUME 1132

POLITICS AND POLICY IN AMERICAN INSTITUTIONS

STEVEN A. SHULL, *Series Editor*

PRESIDENTS AS CANDIDATES
*Inside the White House
for the Presidential Campaign*
Kathryn Dunn Tenpas

PRESIDENTS AS CANDIDATES
INSIDE THE WHITE HOUSE
FOR THE PRESIDENTIAL CAMPAIGN

KATHRYN DUNN TENPAS

GARLAND PUBLISHING, INC.
A MEMBER OF THE TAYLOR & FRANCIS GROUP
NEW YORK AND LONDON
1997

Library of Congress Cataloging-in-Publication Data

Tenpas, Kathryn Dunn.
    Presidents as candidates : inside the White House for the presidential
campaign / by Kathryn Dunn Tenpas.
        p.   cm. — (Garland reference library of social science ; v. 1132.
Politics and policy in American institutions ; v. 1)
    Includes bibliographical references and index.
    ISBN 0-8153-2506-1 (alk. paper)
    1. Presidents—United States—Election.   2. Electioneering—United
States.   3. Incumbency (Public officers)—United States.   4. Presidents—
United States—Staff—Political activity.   5. Campaign management—United
States.   I. Title.   II. Series: Garland reference library of social science ; v.
1132.   III. Series: Garland reference library of social science. Politics and
policy in American institutions ; v. 1.
JK528.T46   1997
324.7'0973—dc21   97-18440
                                                                        CIP

Cover photograph of the White House used with the permission of the
White House Historical Society.

Printed on acid-free, 250-year-life paper
Manufactured in the United States of America

For Ron

Contents

Series Editor's Foreword

It is with great pleasure that we introduce the inaugural volume in the Garland series "Politics and Policy in American Institutions." The series strives to show the interaction of American political institutions within the context of public policymaking. A public policy approach often by definition is all encompassing. Admittedly, my own interests focus on national policymaking, but the series will also include works on all levels of government. Indeed, I do not want my own specialties to define the series. Therefore, we seek solid scholarship incorporating a wide range of actors, including those outside the usual definition of government actors. The policy concerns, too, are potentially quite broad, with special interests in the policy process and such substantive issue areas as foreign and defense policy, economic and budget policy, health care, social welfare, racial politics and the environment. The series will publish a considerable range of works, ranging from upper division to scholarly monographs, including both hard and soft cover editions.

Presidents as Candidates offers a truly unique treatment of the White House role in the reelection efforts of contemporary presidents since 1956. Throughout the volume, Kathryn Tenpas compares and contrasts these eight reelection efforts (from Eisenhower through Clinton). She considers the many unique differences and similarities of each White House–led effort. As with any good study, she considers the multitude of political, institutional and policy factors (domestic, economic and international) that affect the strategies and decisions made. She then develops a typology of three standard types of campaigns—victorious, defeated and takeover—that proves useful in understanding the reelection efforts. Tenpas's book is invaluable in that it allows us, as she states, to "better understand the role of 'president as candidate' as well as its impact on the institutionalized presidency." In that sense, the volume represents an important contribution to our understanding of the modern presidency by explaining presidential reelection campaigns from the White House perspective.

I recognized early on the value of Kathryn Tenpas's volume, with her mixture of approaches, incorporating relevant theory, elite interviews, comparative case studies and quantitative analysis where appropriate. Her book is scholarly but should also appeal to a wider audience than only presidential election scholars because of its subject matter and her deft combination of journalistic and scholarly research. From her vantage point as a UVA graduate student, she was able to interview 53 experts, representing participants from the various administrations. Overall, she observes that "formal rules, changes in the presidential nominating process, the general decline of political parties and the president's statutory ability to expand the White House staff have all facilitated the shift to a White House–centered campaign." She finds that the management of presidential campaigns has been fundamentally altered through centralization of efforts within the White House itself. *Presidents as Candidates* concludes that "during a reelection year, the business of governing is set aside for the business of campaigning."

Steven A. Shull

Acknowledgments

The many years of research and writing that have created this book have left in their wake a multitude of debts to supportive friends, loving family members, inspirational teachers and helpful colleagues and mentors. The starting point for this book was undoubtedly Georgetown Professor James Lengle, whose enthusiasm for presidential electoral politics prompted me to pursue graduate studies so that I might learn more about the subject. The guidance and generosity of Charles Jones, James Ceaser, Steve Finkel and Larry Sabato expanded my initial interest in campaigns to a broader interest in American institutions. The idea for this book, however, emerged from an impromptu meeting with Charles Jones in a Charlottesville bagelry when he off-handedly mentioned that one area in the literature that had gone relatively unnoticed, despite its important implications for governing, was the notion of presidents as candidates.

From that opening bagel to this book, I received a great deal of support from the University of Virginia, the Bradley Foundation, and the Brookings Institution, where I conducted the bulk of my research. While at Brookings I learned much outside the confines of my office from Bob Katzmann, Kent Weaver, Stephen Hess, Bert Rockman, Tom Mann and Pietro Nivola. Research fellows Matthew Dickinson, Charles Shipan and Forrest Maltzman demonstrated a great deal of patience in helping me think through difficult arguments and issues. Additionally, I am deeply grateful to the many former White House and party staff members who generously gave of their time to speak with me, and also to the helpful staff at the Carter Library, the Nixon Collection of the National Archives, the Ford Library, the Johnson Library and the Miller Center at the University of Virginia. All provided critical research assistance in a kindly manner. I am also indebted to Galen Irwin, Peter Mair and Rudy Andeweg of Leiden University in The Netherlands. They provided me with a year's worth of splendid colleagueship and international perspective. So too did my Norwegian officemate, Hanne Marthe Narud, who broadened my horizons by teaching me the wonders of coalition politics in western Europe. Colleagues from the Department of Government and International Affairs at the University of South Florida also provided ongoing moral support and encouragement in the final stages of the project while Adam Newmark provided expert research assistance.

I was very fortunate to have worked with Garland series editor Steven Shull, whose comments and criticism enhanced the final product. Thanks also to David Estrin and the professional staff at Garland Publishing, whose kind assistance simplified the production process.

As all authors know, however, it is the support of family and friends that enables one to complete such an extensive, often frustrating, but ultimately rewarding, project. My parents, brothers and sister provided steady encouragement despite their puzzlement at the seemingly endless parade of revisions. At those times when I could no longer see any light at the end of the tunnel, Bruce Bimber and Jessica Korn provided that essential flicker through their unflagging support and friendship. Thanks to old friends in Washington—Steve Dunne, Renee Stone (who also shared her excellent editing skills), Marya Stark, Kathi Reidy and Margaret Edgell—who provided the all-important free lodging and entertainment during my research trips. And I am forever grateful to my husband Ron for providing encouragement, wise judgment and keen insight. As always, I am ultimately responsible for any shortcomings or errors present in this book.

Presidents as Candidates
Inside the White House for the Presidential Campaign

During the 1992 presidential campaign, President Bush announced, "I will do what I have to do to be reelected."[1] While it is not clear what George Bush would have had to do to secure reelection, his willingness to do whatever necessary was apparent. But what does this mean? We know that during the presidential reelection campaign, the chief executive must take on the dual role of president and candidate as he engages in a nationwide election campaign. But how do presidents prepare for the forthcoming election, manage a nationwide campaign and fulfill presidential duties?

Since 1956, Lyndon Johnson has been the only president who declined to run for another term; seven out of eight sitting presidents have sought to renew their lease on the White House. Though campaigning for reelection has become a staple of the modern presidency, there is scant academic scholarship explaining how presidents prepare and run for reelection. Students of presidential campaigns and the presidency have tended to treat the campaign solely as an electoral phenomenon–assessing the selection process, analyzing fundraising efforts or evaluating campaign strategy. In an attempt to expand our understanding of modern presidential campaigns and the presidency, this study examines presidential reelection campaigns from the vantage point of the White House. It explains how presidents manage their reelection campaign and, in the process, sheds light on how the quest for reelection affects White House operations in the short-term as well as governance more generally. For example, in discussing George Bush's electoral defeat in 1992, former Press Secretary Marlin Fitzwater commented, "We didn't shut the White House down like we should have."[2] Such a statement teaches us much about the management of modern presidential campaigns in that it reveals the White House–centered nature of these events. In addition, this declaration provides much instruction about the focus of government during a reelection year. Fitzwater's comment implies that the White House must "shut down" its typical functions in order to prepare for the campaign, thereby suggesting that governing takes a back-seat to campaigning.

In my study, I focus on eight presidential campaigns, beginning in 1956: Eisenhower '56, Johnson '64, Nixon '72, Ford '76, Carter '80, Reagan '84, Bush '92 and Clinton '96.[3] These cases include those presidents who sought *reelection* as well as those who simply sought *election* (Johnson '64 and Ford '76).

While it is not surprising that the eight presidential campaigns addressed in this study are not identical, *how* and *why* do they vary? There are a number of factors which affect a single presidential reelection campaign: the president's public standing, international crises, the state of the economy, internal party cohesion, opposition party activity, presidential personality and style, the influence of key advisers and the caliber of the opponent. And whether a president confronts an international crisis will also influence how he will campaign, just as the presence of a primary challenge will force presidents to move into candidate mode sooner than they might like. Presidents who face a troubled economy will choose a campaign strategy focusing on the future rather than one that touts their record as president. Presidents who lack a primary challenge will stay safely ensconced in the White House and frame their strategy around the general election and likely nominee. These are many, but certainly not all, of the variables affecting a president's reelection campaign. And since 1956, variation across reelection campaigns is the rule, not the exception.

Common patterns, however, have emerged since 1956 and it is possible to develop a typology based primarily on election outcome and candidate background. Three standard types of presidential reelection campaigns emerge: Victorious Presidents (Eisenhower, Nixon, Reagan and Clinton), Defeated Presidents (Carter and Bush) and Takeover Presidents (Johnson and Ford). Though different in fundamental ways, these campaigns share some striking similarities that are worthy of identification.

TYPE 1: VICTORIOUS PRESIDENTS

These presidents shared the common features of increasing public approval ratings, the absence of a viable primary challenger and a well-organized campaign operation. In each case, the president's approval rating increased in the year of the reelection campaign. This upward trend bodes well for a president seeking reelection for it reflects a strength that is difficult for a challenger to overcome. For example, generally high approval ratings also signal a relatively stable economy and effectively rule out the possibility that the challenger can claim to save the economy from depression or inflation. Strong approval ratings also dissuade intraparty challengers which eliminates a major burden for the incumbent.

As the following chapters explain in detail, each of these presidents possessed an experienced, well-oiled campaign operation that initiated its campaign planning well in advance of the election and, because of the absence of a primary challenge, could focus its efforts on the general election. Advance planning is critical to a successful reelection campaign and, as such, is the hallmark of each of the victorious presidents.

TYPE 2: DEFEATED PRESIDENTS

These presidential reelection campaigns are characterized by declining approval ratings, the presence of a viable primary challenger, and, in some cases, a disorganized reelection organization. While a decline in public approval is reflective of a number of factors (all of which do not bode well for the incumbent), the presence of a primary challenge signals intraparty dissension. More often than not, however, the primary challenge reflects the dissatisfaction of a particular wing of the party. In the case of President Carter, the liberal wing of the party, represented by Senator Ted Kennedy, was angry at the Carter administration for what it perceived as an abandonment of liberal policy positions. Similarly, President Bush faced a challenge from the conservative wing of the Republican party which was annoyed with the Bush presidency for its moderate approach to policymaking and virtual abandonment of the Reagan agenda.

In the case of President Carter, the presence of the Iranian hostage crisis also had a major impact on his reelection campaign. In many cases, a crisis overseas can cause voters to "rally around the flag" in support of the president, but a crisis that dragged on for as long as it did during the Carter administration raised questions about the president's ability to handle the job.[4]

While President Bush did not confront a crisis of that magnitude, he did suffer repeated allegations of a disorganized campaign organization, a faltering economy and a presidency that neglected domestic policy. The culmination of these factors is perhaps best reflected in President Bush's dramatically declining public approval ratings in the last year of his administration.

Neither the primary challenges of Kennedy or Buchanan posed real threats to the convention outcome, but their presence put the presidents on the defensive, labeled them as candidates well before election day and drained finite resources from the presidential campaign. Perhaps the worst side effect of a primary challenger is that he or she emphasizes the president's vulnerabilities at the worst possible time. As a result, presidents facing a serious primary challenge have no choice but to abandon their coveted high ground in the White House and attack.

TYPE 3: TAKEOVER PRESIDENTS[5]

This category is reserved for those presidents who inherited the office by virtue of serving as vice president and, for the purposes of this study, consists of Presidents Johnson and Ford. It is vital to treat these campaigns separately:

> Voters do not elect them as presidents; they did not elect Ford as vice president. . . . Their advantages and disadvantages are traceable to the man they succeeded. To create their own presidency they had to work through and around the direct legacy of their predecessor.[6]

These unelected presidents confronted a completely different strategic context because of the circumstances under which they assumed office. As this book makes quite clear in forthcoming chapters, the quest for reelection requires a great deal of early planning and effort, not to mention a record of accomplishments upon which to run. Candidates who lack the time to create a record of achievements and the opportunity to run a national campaign, like Ford and to a lesser degree, Johnson, are at a distinct disadvantage. Keep in mind that while takeover presidents were never elected to the presidency, they face the same electoral demands as their immediate predecessor.

And yet even making this distinction of the Takeover President is not enough, as Presidents Johnson and Ford provide a marked contrast in the type of reelection campaigns they conducted. For even among takeover presidents, the conditions under which they assumed the presidency had a profound impact on their campaign. In Johnson's case, he became president as a result of a tragedy which gripped the nation, the assassination of President John F. Kennedy. Thus, his quest for the presidency less than one year later was largely shaped by this event. The electorate was saddened at the premature and tragic death of their leader and eager to see the Kennedy agenda enacted. According to Charles O. Jones, such circumstances served Johnson well, "He [Johnson] was free to prepare for the 1964 presidential election by seeking to move as much legislation as possible in the time he had available. He was uniquely equipped to do just that."[7]

On the other hand, President Ford faced a much less favorable political climate. Assuming the presidency on the heels of Watergate, perhaps the greatest political scandal that this country has ever witnessed, President Ford confronted an angry and cynical electorate frustrated with politics as usual. Compounding these problems were the disastrous midterm elections in which the Republicans lost forty-three seats in the House and three in the Senate, Ford's lack of national campaign experience and, perhaps most significantly, his pardon of President Nixon. So while Presidents Johnson and Ford are grouped together because both were unelected presidents, the context under which they inherited the office varied and dramatically influenced their reelection prospects.

The variation across presidential reelection campaigns lies in the fact that each president confronts a unique strategic context, one that is largely influenced by major institutional developments that have occurred in presidential campaigns over the past forty years. Chapter One demonstrates that since Eisenhower's reelection campaign in 1956, control over the presidential campaign has shifted from the party organization to the White House. A systematic study reveals that formal rules changes in the presidential nominating process, the general decline of political parties and the president's statutory ability to expand the White House staff have all facilitated the shift to a White House–centered presidential campaign.[8] These developments are significant in that they have fundamentally altered the management of presidential reelection campaigns.

Chapter Two systematically examines the mechanics and management of the president's reelection campaign—more specifically the role of the White House. Who participates in campaign planning? When does the White House staff begin preparing for the campaign and in what activities do they partake in order to prepare for the campaign? Answers to these questions not only illuminate Mr. Fitzwater's comment about "shutting down the White House," but also expand our understanding of the modern president in his dual role as president and candidate.

Recognizing the central role of the White House, Chapter Three asks the question, *what changes* when the campaign begins? My study reveals that there are six short-term effects brought on by the presidential campaign. For example, there is evidence that the presidential campaign precipitates a White House staff restructuring or reorganization prior to or during the campaign season. Typically, during the third year of the president's first term, staff members begin to prepare for the campaign by moving to the campaign headquarters or expanding their responsibilities within the White House.[9] The presidential campaign also alters the amount and substance of staff work, politicizes the decision-making process to an even greater degree, decreases presidential policy initiative, and alters presidential and cabinet activity as they engage in numerous campaign speeches, debates, fundraising events, and increasing domestic travel. Tracking the timing and scope of these election-year effects over the course of the president's first term explains the impact of the simultaneous management of the government and the presidential campaign. In short, it demonstrates how campaigning gradually assumes front and center stage on the presidential agenda. This is not to say that the business of governing is ignored, only that campaigning has a dramatic impact on White House decision-making and operations.

Any discussion of the president's reelection campaign would be incomplete if it did not address the functions of the campaign committee and the national party organization (Republican National Committee, RNC, and Democratic National Committee, DNC). Both play important roles in the presidential campaign and since 1956, their efforts have been increasingly controlled by the White House. Not surprisingly, then, the activities of the campaign organization and party are far from autonomous. Chapters Four and Five discuss each of these campaign participants and, in the process, demonstrate their variable influence within the president's reelection campaign. These two chapters round out the discussion of the mechanics of presidential reelection campaigns.

Chapter Six assesses the implications of these findings for the various institutions of government and governance more generally. Understanding how presidents run their presidential campaign provides a wealth of information and confirms some of what we may already think about the institution of the presidency, White House staff and political parties. For example, based upon what we know about the twentieth-century development of the Office of the President, it is not at all surprising that the White House, in effect, "manages" the presidential campaign. The institutionalized presidency, characterized by specialization and centralization, has increasingly internalized policymaking and politics within the White House and the reelection campaign is yet another manifestation of this development. Since campaigning for reelection is common practice among today's presidents, students of the presidency should be aware of the toll that campaigning takes on governing, and ultimately on the institution of the presidency.

And finally, the epilogue is a memorandum to the next president, drawing special attention to "what works and what doesn't" in presidential reelection campaigns. The book's overview of the eight most recent reelection campaigns provides the necessary background for a discussion of a successful reelection campaign and offers tips for positioning the president's reelection campaign. Given the increasing uncertainty of renomination and reelection these days, such advice may not only prove to be worthwhile to incumbents, but interesting to spectators as well.

STUDYING PRESIDENTS AS CANDIDATES

Some observers of the presidency are quick to argue that the president campaigns for reelection from day one and that everything he does is solely for the sake of being reelected. According to this school of thought, it would then be impossible to explain how presidents prepare for reelection because there is no separation between the business of governing and reelection politics. Certainly there are difficulties in studying an institution which is inherently political since there is some degree of similarity between the politics of governing and campaigning.[10] Both involve bargaining and coalition-building, two common presidential activities.

Despite such overt similarity, however, there are concrete activities that are exclusively campaign-oriented tasks. For instance, appointing an individual from the White House or the Cabinet to manage the independent presidential campaign organization, filing a statement of candidacy with the Federal Election Commission (FEC) and participating in campaign strategy meetings are all concrete activities that can be observed in presidential reelection campaigns. My study demonstrates that it is possible to point to specific campaign-related tasks that occur over the course of the president's first term in office. Assuming this to be correct, additional research can then identify the point at which campaign planning begins, the participants involved and how this event alters White House operations in the short term.

I utilize a comparative case study technique drawing on over fifty interviews with former White House staff members and national party staff members, documents from presidential libraries, periodicals and secondary sources pertaining to the various presidential campaigns. Case studies include Presidents Eisenhower through Clinton—cases in which presidents served a complete term before seeking reelection as well as those presidents who served partial terms. Johnson's effort in 1964 is noted despite the unique circumstances surrounding his ascension to office and the brevity of his term. The Ford administration suffered from defects similar to the 1964 Johnson campaign (unusual circumstances in coming to office, abbreviated tenure) but, as with Johnson, aspects of his presidential bid are relevant.

At the outset, it is important to clarify various terms mentioned throughout the book. The term "presidency" refers not just to the individual president, but to the president, the Cabinet and the White House staff. A statement by Gerald Ford supports this definition: "A Presidency really is a combination of the individual President and his staff."[11] Thus the findings point more broadly to how White House operations change in the short term as a result of campaign preparation, rather than how the president himself or the executive branch changes.

Second, the terms "long-term" and "short-term campaign planning" are used throughout the text. Long-term campaign planning refers to campaign planning prior to the establishment of the president's campaign organization. Such long-term planning is a crucial component of any campaign. According to a Ford staff memorandum, "The success of this campaign will in very large measure be determined by the quality of early planning. . . . Adequate planning time is mandatory for the organizational structuring and political decision-making required for a successful nationwide campaign."[12] Though long-term planning may be difficult to accomplish because of competing priorities, incumbent presidents seeking reelection can and do prepare for the forthcoming campaign. Short-term campaign planning refers to planning subsequent to the formation of the president's personal campaign organization. Such planning reflects the joint effort between the White House and the president's campaign organization as well as the party's involvement in the campaign.

SUMMARY

It was not until the turn of the century that presidents began to campaign on their own behalf. As one scholar describes it, the noncampaigning president first began to disappear when

> Theodore Roosevelt emerged as the paradigmatic twentieth-century president, charming the people with his energy and his personality. Still it was considered undignified to campaign from the White House. Aware that silence would be expected during his 1904 effort, President Roosevelt made lengthy speaking tours in 1902 and 1903.[13]

By 1916, Woodrow Wilson had become the first sitting president to campaign for himself during the general election.[14] Since then, advancements in communications and campaign technology as well as heightened public expectations have permitted ever growing presidential involvement in their own campaigns. The 1992 campaign brought such activity to even greater levels as witnessed by the appearance of presidential candidates on daytime talk-shows, MTV and late night entertainment programs. And in 1996, the campaigns found their way into cyberspace with each candidate creating home pages on the World Wide Web. There is no reason to expect this trend of increasing exposure to reverse itself. And it is a trend with important implications for the presidency given that it is only in the rarest of circumstances that presidents do not seek a second term (e.g., Johnson in 1968).

This book represents an important contribution in that it expands our understanding of the modern presidency by explaining presidential reelection campaigns from the White House perspective. Findings presented in this book demonstrate that during an election year, the business of governing is set aside for the business of campaigning. To date, however, a systematic understanding of how campaigning intrudes on governing has yet to emerge. This book attempts to fill that void by explaining modern trends in the management of presidential reelection campaigns, the mechanics of the president's reelection campaign and the associated implications for governance. With this analysis in hand, students can better understand the role of "president as candidate" as well as its impact on the institution of the presidency.

NOTES

1. Ann Devroy, "New Hampshire Awaits Latest Edition of Candidate Bush," *The Washington Post*, January 15, 1992, p.A1. Ann Devroy was quoting a statement made by President Bush in an interview with David Frost.

2. Interview with Marlin Fitzwater, May 19, 1994.

3. This study excludes "non-reelection" campaigns (1968, 1988), but acknowledges their importance for testing the arguments in this book. In regard to the 1968 election, a modest amount of campaign planning occurred in the Johnson administration prior to his withdrawal from the race in March of 1968. Thus, information regarding the Johnson reelection effort in 1968 is included to the degree that it is applicable.

4. See John Mueller for a discussion of "rally events," *War, Presidents and Public Opinion*, New York: Wiley, 1970, pp.208–213.

5. The term "takeover president" is borrowed from Charles O. Jones. See *The Presidency in a Separated System*, Washington, D.C.: The Brookings Institution, 1994, p.41.

6. Ibid, p.38.

7. Ibid, p.37.

8. Note that this does not mean that the White House single-handedly runs the reelection campaign, but that it has the dominant role in the reelection

campaign. There are some reelection-related tasks which the White House cannot perform (fundraising, coordinating state field campaign organizations), so the president's personal campaign organization (e.g. Bush/Quayle '92) fulfills these purely "campaign-related" tasks. Nonetheless, the White House has the upper hand in the "macro" aspects of the presidential campaign: determining campaign strategy, candidate scheduling and resource allocation.

9. Staff shuffling is not limited to the White House, of course; note that members of executive agencies also leave their positions to work on the campaign. Frequently they earned their appointments by first serving on the president's previous campaign for the presidency. See Dana Priest, "Bureaucrats Are Jumping Ship of State," *The Washington Post*, June 18, 1992, p. A21. See also, "The Movable Brigade," by Graeme Browning in the *National Journal*, October 24, 1992, p.2417. This article documents the "revolving door" between government work and campaign work utilized by over three dozen Bush/Quayle campaign operatives. The author raises the question of whether such frequent turnover negatively affects bureaucratic performance.

10. See Samuel Kernell, "Campaigning, Governing and the Contemporary Presidency," in John Chubb and Paul E. Peterson, *The New Direction in American Politics*, Washington, D.C.: The Brookings Institution, 1985, p.137.

11. Gerald Ford, "Imperiled Not Imperial," *Time*, November 10, 1980, p.31.

12. "Memorandum to the President, from Jack Calkins and Gwen Anderson," April 28, 1975, p.1; obtained from the Gerald R. Ford Library, Cheney 18, "PFC-EXT 5/75/21."

13. Gil Troy, *See How They Ran*, New York: Macmillan, 1991, p. 212, adjacent picture caption.

14. Ibid at p. 2 of picture section, see caption.

PRESIDENTS
AS CANDIDATES

CHAPTER 1

Managing the President's Campaign
Its Evolution 1956–1996

Modern day incumbent presidential campaigns are no longer dependent on the party organization. This emancipation has prompted presidents to rely instead on their personal staff and an independent campaign organization (e.g. Carter/Mondale '80, Bush/Quayle '92). Of the eight presidents under study, Eisenhower is the only president who allowed the national party to play a pivotal role in the reelection campaign. The declining role of the political party and the expanding role of the White House in the president's campaign have permanently altered the management of the incumbent's campaign. This chapter examines the evolution of the reelection campaign and, in the process, draws attention to significant electoral and institutional developments since 1956.

PRESIDENTS AS CANDIDATES SINCE 1956

Beginning with President Eisenhower's reelection campaign is appropriate since campaigning for the presidency occurred in a very different context than it did for Presidents Nixon through Clinton. Historically, one might in fact make President Eisenhower the dividing point between the old method of campaign organization with the party organization at the helm, and the modern method with the White House and the president's personal campaign organization at the helm. Eisenhower's reelection campaign in 1956 is classified as a "unified" campaign organization, one in which the president runs the campaign through the national party organization that he seeks to direct. According to Ogden and Peterson, the election campaigns of 1936, 1940, 1944, 1948 and 1956 are all examples of a unified campaign organization in which the party and the president's staff were fully integrated into a single campaign organization.[1]

Not only did the RNC run the 1956 reelection campaign, but in the precampaign stages, it pressured President Eisenhower to seek a second term:

> Whatever doubts may have been in the President's mind, or whatever family pressures may have been brought on him to serve but one term, the official party organization never wavered in its outspoken demand that he should run.[2]

In addition to demanding that the President seek reelection, it was the RNC in 1955 that approved plans for a late convention and a short campaign. The party operation, with Len Hall as the chair of the RNC, continued and expanded Eisenhower's reelection campaign.[3]

> It remains true . . . that the Republican National Committee in the 1956 campaign was probably as well organized and as effective as it ever has been.[4]

Though the independent campaign organization was not a component of Eisenhower's reelection effort, upon closer examination, it appears that the organization of the RNC reflected a classic campaign organization:

> In that campaign Leonard W. Hall [Chair of the RNC] of New York was chairman [of the campaign]. Below Hall several divisions were arranged. The Campaign Division, under the direction of Robert Humphreys, had responsibility for plans, programs, and the implementation of policy incidental to the campaign. The Executive

Division, under the direction of Chauncy Robbins, a veteran national committee staff man, had charge of such matters as patronage and budget . . . *The organization of the Republican National Committee— which in 1956 was the campaign organization—was that simple.*[5]

This campaign was the last of its breed, as subsequent incumbent campaigns gradually moved away from the unified model.[6]

The next sitting president to launch a bid from the White House was Lyndon Johnson in 1964. It is critical to remember, however, that the Johnson campaign in 1964 took place under the cloud of the Kennedy assassination. LBJ, a president unelected in his own right, campaigned extensively in hopes of obtaining a mandate to carry out the Kennedy agenda as well as to establish his Great Society programs. In addition, Johnson was sensitive to the needs of the Kennedy people and was careful not to make drastic alterations.[7] President Johnson allowed many Kennedy and Johnson staff members to participate in "political" activities for the 1964 presidential campaign.[8] Keep in mind, however, that this decision was also intensely strategic:

Needing the Kennedy men in 1964 to help carry the North and East as they needed Johnson and his men in 1960 to help carry the South, President Johnson promptly asked the entire Kennedy team to stay, in the Cabinet, on the White House staff, and at the National Committee.[9]

Thus, the 1964 campaign represents the initial shift away from the unified model of campaign management. Rather than letting the DNC run the campaign, participation involved three different entities: the DNC, the Kennedy holdovers and the Johnson team within the White House.

Johnson, it will be recalled, was again eligible for the presidency in 1968. After he was elected in his own right in 1964, Johnson was essentially free from obligation to the Kennedy holdovers—there would not be a divided staff as there was in the 1964 election. His campaign organization had the potential to become the embryo of future campaigns—a personal campaign organization with peripheral involvement from the party. However, reelection planning for 1968 was stymied by LBJ's "secret" decision not to run. According to Press Secretary George Christian, "The truth is, there wasn't much [campaign] planning going on [because of the possibility of Johnson's withdrawal]."[10] However, the President's senior aide (equivalent to the modern-day chief of staff) Marvin Watson moved down the hall to deal exclusively with reelection planning. Though Watson apparently was aware of LBJ's decision not to run, he doubted that LBJ would stick to this decision and wanted to be prepared. When Johnson finally announced he would not seek reelection, a semblance of a campaign operation already had developed under the auspices of Marvin Watson, and even in its nascent form, it was not a unified campaign organization characterized by extensive involvement from the party organization. Rather, similar to the 1964 campaign, it is likely that the party's role would have been diluted by White House involvement.

President Nixon followed LBJ's practice of utilizing the White House as a means for initiating early campaign planning. In fact, Nixon was the first president to execute fully this method of campaigning for reelection since neither Kennedy nor Johnson sought *reelection* after serving a complete term in office. This development is especially interesting given the fact that Nixon did not follow the path of his former boss, President Eisenhower, who incorporated the RNC in reelection planning. In addition, President Nixon was the first president to establish an independent campaign organization, the Committee for the Re-election of the President (CREEP). As Sidney Milkis argues:

> The complete autonomy of the Committee for the Re-Election of the President (CREEP) from the regular Republican organization in the 1972 campaign was but the final stage of a long process of White House preemption of the national committee's political responsibilities.[11]

The Nixon reelection campaign was the first completely White House–directed reelection campaign and the first campaign to have an independent campaign organization. The direction from White House staff members, primarily Chief of Staff H.R. Haldeman, coupled with the influx of White House staff to the campaign headquarters, demonstrates the dominant White House influence.

The Ford campaign in 1976 continued the trend of White House–dominated campaigns and the establishment of an independent personal campaign organization (despite Ford's initial refusal to establish such an entity). However, President Ford's experience was quite unusual in that his succession to office eleven months before he declared his candidacy for the 1976 presidential election thrust many of his aides, both inside and outside the White House, into campaign planning shortly after they arrived. Further, the likelihood of a tough primary challenge and the compliance and disclosure requirements mandated by new campaign finance laws accelerated and intensified campaign preparation. Nonetheless, the management of the campaign reflected the Nixon campaign in 1972—an independent campaign organization with substantial involvement from the White House.

THE OFFICE OF POLITICAL AFFAIRS: REELECTION POLITICS WHITE HOUSE STYLE, 1978–1996

By the time of the 1980 presidential election, Presidents Nixon and Ford had set the precedent for a White House–directed campaign complete with the establishment of an independent campaign organization. However, midway through President Carter's term, another stage in the development of the White House–dominated reelection campaign emerged with the establishment of a special office that dealt with the earliest stages of reelection planning in addition to other "political" tasks.

During the first two years of Carter's term, there was much criticism about the lack of political sensitivity permeating the White House. The administration was characterized by many observers as a "bunch of political novices." As a result, part way through Carter's first term, he appointed his scheduling deputy, Tim Kraft, to fill the position of Assistant to the President for Political Affairs and Personnel.[12] Kraft met regularly with John White, the Chair of the Democratic Party, and supervised party affairs. Kraft and the political affairs team made a serious effort to sharpen political sensitivities within the executive branch. In addition, Kraft initiated the first campaign planning efforts at the direction of Chief of Staff Hamilton Jordan. While Jordan drafted the first reelection planning memo to the President, he left nuts-and-bolts campaign planning to the Office of Political Affairs and Personnel.[13]

Though President Carter was the first to designate an individual to fulfill these duties, the position, as stated in the *U.S. Government Manual*, was vaguely referred to as Assistant to the President. It was not until President Reagan that this staff member was given a descriptive, formal title and a separate office, Assistant to the President for Political Affairs. Initially, Lyn Nofziger led this office with Ed Rollins and Lee Atwater as his assistants. Nofziger, however, accepted this position contingent on his departure one year later. After the 1980 election victory he intended to return to California, but was asked by Jim Baker to stay on in this capacity.[14] Adhering to his agreement to stay in the White House for one year, Nofziger resigned in 1982, leaving Ed Rollins at the helm and Lee Atwater as his assistant. Under Rollins, there was a staff of roughly fifteen members presiding over political activities. This office also participated in reelection planning as it did in the Carter administration. After the midterm elections, Chief of Staff James Baker, and Deputy Chief of Staff Michael Deaver, along with strategist Stuart Spencer and pollster Robert Teeter, conducted a series of secret meetings settling most of the details of the campaign.[15] At the direction of James Baker, Ed Rollins and Lee Atwater were assigned responsibility for campaign planning efforts. And in the spring of 1983, Ed Rollins and the staff of the Office of Political Affairs left the White House for the Reagan/Bush reelection campaign headquarters.[16]

President Bush broke the trend that began with Jimmy Carter by downplaying the role of the Office of Political Affairs. Instead, he appointed Lee Atwater as Chair of the RNC. Atwater, a veteran of several campaigns and the Reagan Office of Political Affairs, was the campaign manager for Bush's 1988 presidential campaign. Rather than building up the Office of Political Affairs and designating a White House liaison to the RNC, Bush simply appointed a loyalist, known for his vast strategic and political skills, to the RNC. In a sense, President Bush attempted to revert to the "unified" presidential campaign structure utilized by Eisenhower, one in which the party and the president's staff were fully integrated into a single campaign organization. Appointing Atwater allowed Bush to have a reliable contact at the RNC who could assure him the national party was operating according to White House standards and expectations. However, because of a fatal cancer, Atwater did not hold this position long and his successors lacked the personal ties to the president, which many argue are essential for strong leadership. This development ultimately pushed the Office of Political Affairs to the periphery of White House campaign planning, so while it was involved, staff members did not possess as much influence as in prior reelection campaigns. Further, the Bush administration's reluctance to initiate early reelection campaign planning coupled with staffing problems resulted in an ill-coordinated campaign characterized by disarray and disorganization. Nonetheless, the central role of the White House reflected the general trend of reelection campaign management that began with the Nixon administration.

The Office of Political Affairs was both active and influential in the Clinton reelection campaign, despite an inauspicious beginning. By the third year of President Clinton's term, the Office of Political Affairs was seeking its third director. While the first director, Rahm Emanuel, had close ties to Clinton, he resigned due to "personality conflicts," and his successor, Joan Baggett, lacked the access and influence Emanuel possessed. She ultimately resigned after the midterm elections. Her successor, Douglas Sosnick, was strongly supported by the President's chief electoral tactician and Deputy White House Chief of Staff, Harold Ickes. In addition, Sosnick had served as the administrative assistant to the newly appointed DNC Chair, Senator Christopher Dodd. Thus, Sosnick possessed close ties to both senior White House staff members and the DNC. These connections enabled Sosnick to run an influential political operation from the White House. Unlike the Reagan administration, which also possessed an influential and active Office of Political Affairs, the Clinton director remained in the White House rather than moving to the reelection campaign.

So while the Office of Political Affairs appears to be the breeding ground for early campaign planning, its influence and role is largely dependent on White House dynamics and staff politics. Under President Carter, Tim Kraft laid the foundation for the reelection campaign. Likewise, under President Reagan, Ed Rollins initiated campaign planning. However, in the Bush administration, Director Ron Kaufman was not nearly so influential in reelection planning, largely because hopes were initially placed in RNC Chair Lee Atwater. And the Clinton reelection campaign reinstated the Office of Political Affairs' role in early reelection planning. So while there has been some variation in terms of influence, it is clear that the Office of Political Affairs has stepped in to fill a void created by a weakening party organization and a concomitant desire to centralize electoral politics in the White House.[17] The establishment of the Office of Political Affairs represented a forthright effort to internalize political resources and its pivotal role in reelection planning demonstrates the increasing politicization of the White House staff.[18]

Since Eisenhower, there has been an undeniable shift away from a party-run incumbent campaign to one that is directed by the White House and executed through an independent, personal campaign organization. In addition, there has been a steady trend within the White House toward increased specialization, one for which the establishment of the Office of Political Affairs is a prime example. Recognizing these institutional developments, it is equally important to account for them.

WHY THE TREND AWAY FROM A PARTY-RUN REELECTION CAMPAIGN?

As Chapter Five will explain in detail, the national party organization is, in theory, an institution designed to promote the president's reelection campaign, but its role in presidential politics has declined over the past half century. There are two primary reasons for the declining role of the party organization in incumbent presidential campaigns: (1) the expansion of the White House staff and (2) procedural changes/reforms in the presidential electoral process. The president's ability to have a full-time political staff within the White House precluded the need for reliance on the national party's political staff. Furthermore, the rise of primary elections phased out a previously integral role the party played in the nominating process.

Subsequent to the 1937 Brownlow Commission findings, which indicated that the "president needed more help," the president's White House staff gradually expanded.[19] There are a number of reasons for the growth of the White House staff: expansive interest group activity and demands, an expanded U.S. role in international affairs, the growth of government and the increased complexity of public policy. Perhaps an additional reason for White House growth is the ease with which presidents can expand their staff.[20] One method of expanding White House staff is to submit to Congress a reorganization plan that becomes effective sixty days later if there is no formal disapproval registered by a concurrent resolution or a simple resolution. And as Terry Moe points out, such requests are rarely challenged by Congress:

> The answer is rooted in Congress's collective action problems. Legislators do not care much about incremental changes in the institutional presidency unless their constituents are directly affected. There are no interest group 'fire alarms' to prod them into action, no clear electoral benefits to be gained from opposing the president. Meantime, presidents care intensely, and they dedicate their resources to getting what they want.[21]

Presidents can also expand their staff by issuing an executive order, an implied presidential power. While it is fair to say that the expansiveness of government partially accounts for the growth of the executive office, the ease with which presidents can expand their office provides little incentive not to do so.

In any event, with greater size came the ability to assume political responsibilities previously handled by the party. Though the Brownlow recommendations were submitted in 1937, real growth in the actual size of the president's staff was not realized until 1947.[22] This staff development within the White House has permanently altered the party's relationship with the president and ultimately established a buffer between the president and the party. Consider the following quotes:

> There really was not any single manager of the [Johnson 1964] campaign, unless it would be President Johnson himself . . . The Democratic National Committee played practically no role at all in the campaign.
>
> *Jack Valenti, Senior Staff Member, President Johnson*[23]

> Those people around Nixon were not Republicans in the sense of trying to build the party. Their only interest was in reelecting the President . . . As for the Republican National Committee, we were relegated to the back of the bus . . . the truth is we weren't ever on the bus at all.
>
> *Robert Dole, RNC Chair, 1972*[24]

> Every clerk at the White House thinks he knows how to do my job.
>
> *Richard Richards, RNC Chair, 1980–82*[25]

> The strengthening of the White House's own political staff has not met with favor from the National Committee chairmen themselves . . . From his experience, Clark Clifford comments, 'I just have to say to you that I doubt that in . . . [a presidential] election either of the national committees [on an incumbent President's side] plays much of a part. They just don't. It's up to the President and his organization to run the campaign; the committee doesn't really do that.'
>
> *Bradley Patterson, former White House staff member and author*[26]

> We noted that the former practice of the candidate's placing major responsibility on the national chairman has given way in modern times to the frequent relegation of the chairman and national committee staff to a poor place in the shadows.
>
> *Authors Cornelius Cotter and Bernard Hennessy*[27]

These statements reflect a sentiment commonplace among academics, former party staff and even presidential staff. The fact of the matter is, "White House staff assistants now handle many of the political chores once assigned to the national party organization."[28] Prior to this development, presidents relied on the national party apparatus to handle political matters and reelection planning.

As noted above, White House staff expansion was a necessary condition because it gave the White House a greater capacity for activity. But certainly presidents could choose to use such resources for different purposes, leaving the business of campaigning to the party leadership. Perhaps the reason they have not done so is that for the president and his senior staff, the loyalty of White House staff members is preferable to working with a large organization where loyalty to the executive is by no means guaranteed.[29] And so, rather than deal directly with the party organization, presidents have assigned a staff member to supervise party operations and act as liaison to the party organization. As a result, senior White House staff members typically are responsible for managing political operations and party affairs, and are informally delegated the task of party chief. In fact, Carter aide Tim Kraft corroborated this statement when he indicated that the establishment of the Office of Political Affairs and Personnel was "an attempt to provide a more constant liaison with the party and to maintain contact with the political base across the country."[30] Not surprisingly, the people who have directed this office have all possessed a wealth of political and campaign experience: Kraft for President Carter; Nofziger, Rollins, Daniels and Donatelli for President Reagan; Wray, Carney and Kaufman for President Bush; and Emanuel, Baggett and Sosnick for President Clinton. At an earlier point in American political history, their backgrounds, no doubt, would have been well-suited for positions at the RNC or DNC.

A second development, related to the demise of political parties, is the changing nature of the presidential selection process. These changes include technical changes in the electoral process, the rise of primaries, as well as parallel developments like the expansive role of the media and telecommunications, the rise of candidate-centered campaign organizations, the demise of the old-style political machine, public financing of presidential elections, and the emergence of a cadre of presidential "handlers."[31]

Perhaps the most salient technical development affecting the role of the parties is the series of electoral reforms which resulted in an increasing number of primaries and a concomitant decline of the caucus system.[32] Since 1968, the nomination process virtually was released from the hands of party leaders and the results are now largely determined by voters' decisions during the primary season. "By 1976, with primaries dominating the selection process, the party . . . played a minimal role. It was 'the people' that had become the decisive force . . ."[33] As the role of the party declined, party leaders took a back seat to the voting populace. Even before the primary system dominated the nomination process, in the '50s and '60s, the mere existence of primaries coupled with the expansive role of the media supplanted the role of the party. Gone were the days when the party called the shots and essentially controlled the nominating process, particularly when an incumbent president was running.

One symptom of the new "open" system is that incumbents are much more vulnerable to serious challenge. In the 1960s, for example, scholars argued that, "The tradition of renomination for a first-term incumbent is at present so firmly established that only the President, by declination or through his own mistakes, can prevent it from operating."[34] Yet with the changes in the nominating process, just twenty years later such a statement could be rebutted:

> Despite the real advantages of incumbency for a presidential campaign, recent years have shown that renomination is not inevitable. Harry Truman, Lyndon Johnson, Gerald Ford, and Jimmy Carter all faced strong challenges when they sought a new four-year lease on the White House.[35]

The primary system basically relegated the parties to mere hosts of the nominating convention and contributed to the increased competitiveness of the nominating contest.

Political scientist John Hart takes this finding one step further by arguing that the reformed nominating process jeopardized the renomination of the president to the point where presidents are forced to pay attention to the reelection campaign for a longer period of time:

The political affairs unit is a formal recognition of the need for first-term presidents to maintain an experienced and professional campaign organization during that first term to cope with the demands of the new rules of the nomination game.[36]

Hart claims that the Office of Political Affairs is a response to the evolutionary movement from back-room to front-room politics characterized by open nominating systems. Thus, according to this argument, the current nomination process is to blame for the establishment of this overtly political White House office. And similarly, Leon Epstein contends:

Because presidents are nominated and elected by increasingly candidate-centered efforts, they are thought to be more inclined now than earlier to govern through personal helpers and broad public appeals rather than conventional party organizations and their coalitions of interests.[37]

Hart and Epstein both agree that presidents must now keep their campaign organization intact throughout the first term so as to facilitate renomination and a reelection victory.

Given the modern day uncertainty of an incumbent's nomination, the White House is wary of nomination challenges and, where possible, works to control the nominating process. One example of early White House engineering to insure renomination occurred in 1977 when the Winograd Commission met to revise Democratic nominating rules. The rules passed by this commission were strongly influenced by Carter White House staff members: and, the new rules, by all accounts, were ones that best facilitated Carter's renomination.

The Winograd Commission was the only commission to deliberate while a Democratic incumbent was in office. As a result, some of the rules it considered were introduced and pushed by a White House that was both aware of the importance of rules and determined to insure President Carter's renomination in 1980.[38]

One Carter aide described the Winograd Commission as "a bunch of party rules freaks who took the lead from the White House."[39] A participant from the DNC claimed that the commission was ". . . all White House directed. Morley Winograd took directions from the White House."[40] The outcome of the Winograd Commission is a telling demonstration both of the dominant role of the White House in reelection planning and the decline of political parties.

And, more recently, the Clinton administration, in an attempt to fend off any primary challenges, ". . . put in place one of the earliest and most aggressive reelection campaigns ever, and its first goal seems to be to scare off—or beat—a Democratic challenger."[41] Clinton strategists realized the combined importance of early fundraising and organizing in a "front-loaded" nominating system—a situation in which numerous states moved up the date of their contests so that by the end of March 1996, 38 states had already held their primary or caucus. Under the front-loaded nominating process, there was little time to recover from a poor showing, let alone time for raising additional money or setting up a field organization. In order to be fully prepared, the Clinton campaign raised more than $10 million by August of 1995.[42]

In conjunction with the changing rules of the game, the media has stepped in to influence and communicate with the electorate and has eliminated the party's role as the conduit to the voters. Rather than grass-roots campaign strategies, primary campaigns require much broader-based efforts that often are media-dominated. The media, not party officials, emerged as the vehicle to influence voters. "Without the mass media, the vast increase of popular influence on the nominating process would have been impossible."[43] The media play a critical role in determining a candidate's popular image, and consequently, candidates bypass the party in order to adjust to the new "communicator" in presidential electoral politics.[44]

Developments altering the presidential electoral process have no doubt weakened the role of the party. Whatever void the party created in terms of campaigning and political maneuvering was filled by the president and his staff. A number of reasons account for the party's declining role in the incumbent's campaign: voters have lost their psychological attachment to political parties; political reforms and increasing population growth have rendered party machines and grass-roots campaigning obsolete; the expansion of government-sponsored social programs have replaced the party's role as provider; and, notable events like Vietnam and Watergate have caused core party members to disaffiliate. Such a state of affairs is not solely due to the candidate-centered nature of current campaigns. Rather, it is a symptom of the larger problems that confront America's two major parties. According to Stephen Hess:

> It is doubtful that American political parties can ever regain the influence they had in the nineteenth century. Government has replaced them as dispenser of social services, patronage is no longer an attractive lure to recruit political workers, a permanent career service now fills all but the top jobs in government, different forms of entertainment and voluntary associations compete with the parties on unequal terms, and television gives the voters increased possibilities to get information and judge candidates outside the party contest. [45]

Given the adverse environment in which political parties operate and compete, it is not at all surprising that the national party organization plays a peripheral role in the incumbent's campaign. The large number of factors affecting the role of the party organization make it difficult to pinpoint which development wreaked the most havoc on the party's role in presidential politics. Certainly one can say that the simultaneous major developments of staff expansion and the rise in primaries were mutually reinforcing. Ultimately, they pushed the party to the periphery of presidential electoral politics. In the current era, presidents call on the party in those limited number of cases where the party can serve the White House. It is a rare day when the president unilaterally offers his services to strengthen the party. Rarer still are occasions when the party imposes itself or its views on the president. In short, as Harmel notes, for modern presidents, self-interest, not altruism, motivates presidential involvement with the party organization.[46]

   Advocates of an active and influential party organization may find such a development disturbing because they yearn for the days of party bosses, back-room deals and grass-roots activism. They may argue that a president free from party constraints is out of touch with the party he claims to represent in the national political arena, and such estrangement is unhealthy for democracy. Additionally, the president's estrangement from the party may further complicate his ability to obtain support in Congress as well as the electorate. Furthermore, the neglect demonstrated by some modern presidents only exacerbates the demise of parties and contributes to a low morale problem among national party employees and party activists.

CONCLUSION

Since President Eisenhower's reelection bid in 1956, the roles of the party and the White House changed dramatically as the modern incumbent presidential campaign became dominated by the White House. The party organization was pushed to the periphery of electoral politics. President Nixon set the stage for White House domination of the reelection campaign by establishing an independent campaign organization. And since President Carter's reelection campaign in 1980, the White House Office of Political Affairs emerged as an internal source of campaign planning. Just as the White House sought to gain increasing control over the policymaking and appointments process, so too it has sought to gain increasing control over campaign politics and management.[47] Of course there are different reasons for these trends, but the underlying pattern of an expansive White House staff seeking control over various aspects of governing and politics remains the same. It is equally important to note that due to the aforementioned institutional developments, electoral competition for the presidency has been in a constant state of change since Eisenhower was reelected in 1956. As a result, presidents have closely monitored these institutional developments and created a reelection campaign apparatus suitable for competition—an apparatus centrally controlled by the White House.

NOTES

1. Daniel M. Ogden, Jr. and Arthur L. Peterson, *Electing the President: 1964*, San Francisco: Chandler Publishing Company, 1964, p. 71.

2. Charles A.H. Thompson and Frances M. Shattuck, *The 1956 Presidential Campaign*, Washington, D.C.: The Brookings Institution, 1960, pp. 13–14.

3. Previously, Len Hall was a Member of Congress who served a stint at the RNC as chair of the National Republican Congressional Committee. In 1953, Hall assumed the position as chair of the RNC on the heels of a scandal involving the previous chair. Ibid, p. 7.

4. Cornelius P. Cotter and Bernard C. Hennessy, *Politics Without Power*, New York: Atherton Press, 1964, p. 126.

5. Ibid, p. 126, (emphasis added).

6. This model is best exemplified during the Roosevelt administration when DNC Chairs James Farley, Edward Flynn and Robert Hannegan took full responsibility for managing FDR's three reelection campaigns. Eugene H. Roseboom, *A History of Presidential Elections*, London: The Macmillan Company, 1970, pp. 454–487.

7. See Karl A. Lamb and Paul A. Smith, *Campaign Decision-Making*, Belmont, CA: Wadsworth Publishing, 1968, p. 153.

8. If President Kennedy had not been assassinated, Larry O'Brien (Congressional Relations), Kenneth O'Donnell (Scheduling) and brother, Robert Kennedy (Attorney General) were to have played leading roles in the reelection campaign. Rowland Evans and Robert Novak, *Lyndon B. Johnson*, New York: The New American Library, 1966, p. 466.

9. Ibid, p. 80.

10. Telephone interview with George Christian, July 7, 1992. See also George Christian, "The Night Lyndon Quit," *Texas Monthly*, April, 1988, p. 109.

11. Sidney M. Milkis, "The Presidency and Political Parties," in Michael Nelson, *The Presidency and the Political System*, (3rd Ed.), Washington, D.C.: Congressional Quarterly, 1990, p. 364.

12. Kraft did not assume this position until 1978 when the Carter administration began to centralize its authority and control over the Cabinet. See Dom Bonafede, "Carter Sounds Retreat from 'Cabinet Government'," *National Journal*, November 18, 1978, p. 1852.

13. For a thorough analysis of the Office of Political Affairs, see Kathryn Dunn Tenpas, "Institutionalized Politics: The White House Office of Political Affairs," *Presidential Studies Quarterly* 26:2, Spring 1996, pp. 511–522.

14. Information obtained in an interview with Lyn Nofziger, May 23, 1994.

15. Michael Deaver's vague title requires further explanation. According to the *National Journal,* "He helps plan Reagan's public appearances and statements, and it is he who helps craft the artful explanations designed to allow the President to insist that his basic principles stand firm despite policy shifts to gain tactical advantages." Dick Kirschten, "President Reagan After Two Years—Bold Actions But Uncertain Results," *National Journal,* January 1, 1983, p. 15.

16. The exodus by Director Rollins and the Office of Political Affairs is reflected in successive editions of the *U.S. Government Manual*; the office is listed in the '82–'83 volume, but deleted in the following edition, the year of the presidential election. Thereafter, it is listed again.

17. John Hart, *The Presidential Branch,* New Jersey: Chatham House Publishers, 1995, p. 128.

18. See Richard W. Waterman, "Closing the Expectations Gap: The Presidential Search for New Political Resources," in Richard W. Waterman (ed.), *The Presidency Reconsidered,* Itasca, IL: F.E. Peacock Publishers, 1993, pp. 38–40. See also Tenpas, "Institutionalized Politics: The White House Office of Political Affairs."

19. See E.O. 8248 and Reorganization Plan I issued under the authority granted Franklin Roosevelt by the 1939 Reorganization Act. For an overview of the White House staff organization and expansion from Hoover through Johnson, see Charles E. Walcott and Karen M. Hult, *Governing the White House,* Lawrence, KS: University Press of Kansas, 1995.

20. Hart, p. 42.

21. Terry Moe, "The Presidency and the Bureaucracy: The Presidential Advantage," in Michael Nelson (ed.), *The Presidency and the Political System,* Washington, D.C.: Congressional Quarterly, 1995, p. 425.

22. Hart, pp. 114–116.

23. Emmette S. Redford and Richard T. McCulley, *White House Operations,* Austin: University of Texas Press, 1986, pp. 175–76. Quote taken from an oral history, n. 67 Valenti oral history, 19 February 1971, pp. 10–11.

24. Bradley H. Patterson, Jr., *The Ring of Power,* New York: Basic Books, 1988, p. 229.

25. Paul Taylor and Lou Cannon, "RNC's Embattled Richards Resigns; Timing and Performance Questioned," *The Washington Post*, October 5, 1982, p. A5.

26. Patterson, p. 233.

27. Cotter and Hennessy, p. 125.

28. Michael Nelson (ed.), *Congressional Quarterly's Guide to the Presidency*, Washington, D.C.: Congressional Quarterly Press, 1989, p. 613.

29. This was a particular problem in the Carter administration because there were several pro-Kennedy people sprinkled about the DNC.

30. Telephone interview with Tim Kraft, July 6, 1992.

31. See Leon D. Epstein, *Political Parties in the American Mold*, Madison, WI: University of Wisconsin Press, 1986, pp. 109–111, for a detailed discussion of the development of the candidate-centered campaign.

32. See Paul Herrnson, *Party Campaigning in the 1980's*, Cambridge: Harvard University Press, 1988, p. 1.

33. James W. Ceaser, *Presidential Selection*, Princeton: Princeton University Press, 1979, p. 288. See also Thomas J. Weko, *The Politicizing Presidency*, Lawrence, KS: University Press of Kansas, 1995, pp. 78–80.

34. Paul T. David, Ralph M. Goldman and Richard C. Bain, *The Politics of National Party Conventions*, revised edition, New York: University Press of America, 1964, p. 84.

35. Nelson, (1989), p. 220.

36. Hart, p. 128.

37. Epstein, pp. 113–114.

38. James Lengle, "Democratic Party Reforms: The Past as Prologue to the 1988 Campaign," *The Journal of Law and Politics*, Vol IV, No.2, Fall 1987, p. 242. See also Rhodes Cook, "Democrats Adopt New Rules for Picking Nominee in 1980," *Congressional Quarterly*, June 17, 1978, p. 1571.

39. Off-the-record interview with former Carter staff member.

40. Interview with Elaine Kamarck, July 24, 1991.

41. Ann Devroy, "Clinton: Decisive, Hard-Charging, Goal-Oriented," *The Washington Post National Weekly Edition*, August 14–20, 1995, p. 16.

42. Ibid.

43. David et al., p. 29.

44. For an incisive critique of the media's role as communicator, see Thomas Patterson, *Out of Order*, New York: Random House, 1994.

45. Stephen Hess, *The Presidential Campaign*, (3rd Ed.), Washington, D.C.: The Brookings Institution, 1988, pp. 87–88.

46. Robert Harmel, *Presidents and Their Parties*, New York: Praeger, 1984, p. 251.

47. See Terry Moe, "The Politicized Presidency," in John Chubb and Paul Peterson, *The New Direction in American Politics*, Washington, D.C.: The Brookings Institution, 1985, pp. 235–271. See also Weko, throughout.

CHAPTER 2

Inside the White House for the President's Campaign

Though we know a great deal about the electoral process and the details of various presidential campaigns, surprisingly little analysis has been conducted about how presidents actually prepare for the forthcoming campaign. Cynical observers, like journalist Sidney Blumenthal and former Johnson aide, Jack Valenti, frequently accuse the president of spending the entire first term preparing and campaigning for reelection.[1] This judgment, however, trivializes the activities of the president by failing to recognize the fact that presidents often care about governing despite electoral considerations.

In any case, whatever a president's inclinations, it is frequently difficult to plan ahead given the overwhelming day-to-day demands at the White House. External, unpredictable events also hinder White House efforts to focus on the reelection campaign. As one former staff member explained, "At the White House we had often talked about long-range planning, but we rarely did it—we were almost entirely crisis-oriented."[2] Notwithstanding the fact that presidents sometimes act without regard to their electoral interest, and that planning efforts often go awry, it remains true that one staple of the modern presidency is an attempt to improve the chances for victory by carefully planning the reelection campaign.

This chapter explains how presidents prepare for the reelection campaign by answering three major questions: who participates in campaign planning, when do residents begin preparation for the forthcoming campaign, and in what activities do White House planners partake when preparing for such a campaign? These questions are best explored by studying the campaign planning efforts from Presidents Eisenhower through Clinton. This time period includes modern presidents in the post-war era when telecommunications emerged as an integral component of presidential campaigns. This era is also characterized by extensive changes in the electoral "rules of the game," the introduction of public campaign financing and major technological advancements in the mechanics of presidential campaigns (e.g., in-house polling, direct mail, focus groups).

There are three principal participants in the modern president's campaign: the White House, the party and the campaign organization. Of these, the White House is the most important and, in modern campaigns, dominates campaign planning. As Bradley Patterson aptly states, "When the president runs for reelection, his real campaign headquarters is . . . the White House."[3] And similarly, William Kristol, Vice President Quayle's chief of staff, notes, "When you're an incumbent President . . . the White House is the key decision-making place, not the campaign. . . . "[4] This perception about the White House's integral role in the campaign is commonplace among former White House staff and party members. Set out below is a discussion of this "campaign in the White House."

WHO'S INVOLVED?

When seeking the answer to the question, "Who's involved in campaign planning?," it is difficult to provide a concise response that identifies planners as individuals in specific White House staff positions. The difficulty stems in part from the substantial changes that have occurred in the White House organization since President Eisenhower—the White House staff size has doubled and positions have become more specialized.[5] In addition to the changing nature of the White House staff structure, the president's personality also accounts for variation. The process of naming "politicos" to staff

Sources of Early Reelection Planning in the White House

The Major Players

President	Position	Staff Member
Eisenhower	Chief of Staff	Sherman Adams
	RNC Chair	Leonard Hall
Johnson '68	Scheduling	Marvin Watson
	Senior Aides	Jack Valenti
		Bill Moyers
Nixon	Chief of Staff	H.R. Haldeman
	Communications	Jeb Magruder
	Scheduling	Hugh Sloan
	Recruiting	Harry Fleming
	Attorney General	John Mitchell
	Office of Domestic Affairs	John Ehrlichman
	Counsellor	Robert Finch
		Bryce Harlow
	Special Counsel	Harry Dent
		Charles Colson
		Murray Chotiner
Ford	Chief(s) of Staff	Donald Rumsfeld
		Richard Cheney
	Commerce Dept.	James Baker
	Outside Adviser	Stuart Spencer
Carter	Chief of Staff	Hamilton Jordan
	Office of Political Affairs and Personnel	Tim Kraft
	Press Secretary	Jody Powell
	Communications	Gerald Rafshoon
	Outside Adviser	Pat Caddell
Reagan	Chief of Staff	James Baker
	Deputy Chief of Staff	Michael Deaver
	Deputy to the Chief of Staff	Richard Darman
	Office of Political Affairs	Ed Rollins
		Lee Atwater
	Outside Advisers	Stuart Spencer
		Robert Teeter
Bush	Chief(s) of Staff	Samuel Skinner
		James Baker
	Commerce Dept.	Robert Mosbacher
	Outside Advisers	Fred Malek
		Robert Teeter
Clinton	Chief of Staff	Leon Panetta
	Senior Adviser	George Stephanopoulos
	Deputy Chief of Staff	Harold Ickes
	Director, Office of Political Affairs	Douglas Sosnick
	Outside Adviser	Richard Morris

positions is not an institutionalized phenomenon. While no set pattern exists, it is apparent that campaign planning efforts occur wherever the president's closest political aides are positioned in the White House. For example, if such an aide was thought to perform well in White House scheduling, his source of campaign planning most likely would be the scheduling office. An historical overview demonstrates that no single White House office has a special claim to campaign-related work; rather such work is parceled out to those whom the president trusts regardless of their location in the White House.

Based on numerous interviews, document review and relevant secondary sources, the table on the previous page identifies those who played a major role (part of the inner circle) in early campaign planning, and, in the process, demonstrates the wide range of campaign-related positions within the White House staff structure. Those involved in planning LBJ's 1964 campaign are not listed since there was no opportunity for early planning. Recall that the Kennedy assassination in November of 1963 thrust Johnson into office a mere two months before the presidential primaries began.

An overview of major participants in the president's campaign effort indicates that there is substantial diversity across the various administrations. Despite this variation, the central role of the chief of staff in campaign planning is present in seven of the eight administrations; the exception is President Johnson who did not have a chief of staff. President Johnson relied instead on a handful of senior aides, and among those, Marvin Watson may have been the equivalent of a chief of staff. According to campaign veteran Bob Teeter, "When you have an incumbent President, the chief of staff of the White House in some way has to be the linchpin of whatever is done in the campaign that involves the President."[6]

Indeed, as the previous chart indicates, presidents have relied on their chiefs of staff for guidance and coordination in the reelection campaign. Sherman Adams, Eisenhower's chief of staff, supervised campaign planning for Ike's successful reelection bid. Nixon's chief of staff, H.R. Haldeman, was intimately involved in campaign planning, along with John Mitchell, the Attorney General and close friend of the President. During Ford's brief tenure, Richard Cheney, a very young chief of staff, worked closely with campaign manager James Baker and strategist Stuart Spencer. Similarly, Hamilton Jordan supervised the planning efforts of Tim Kraft and drafted the first memo outlining campaign planning. During the Reagan administration, James Baker participated in the earliest form of campaign planning and supervised the efforts of the Rollins team. In the Bush administration, Chief of Staff Samuel Skinner initially coordinated the members of the president's reelection team, followed by James Baker who took over as chief of staff in the summer of 1992. In the aftermath of the 1992 campaign, the White House liaison to the '84 campaign, Margaret Tutwiler, stated:

> That particular election, like this one, was run out of the Chief of Staff's office at the White House. It happens to have been the same person in both instances, Jim Baker. Everybody else knew who had the final say and who ran the campaigns. Dick Cheney ran President Ford's campaign out of the Chief of Staff's office. You have to if you're a sitting president. [7]

And in the Clinton reelection campaign, Chief of Staff Leon Panetta played an integral role in reelection planning. Such a finding is not surprising given the traditional significance of the chief of staff's role and the importance of reelection to the president.[8]

While the chart at the beginning of this section demonstrates the diversity in sources of campaign planning, interesting trends emerge. In three of the last four presidential reelection campaigns, the logistics of campaign planning were handled by members of the Office of Political Affairs. Tim Kraft of the Carter administration worked on the early aspects of campaign planning and eventually moved over to the Carter/Mondale campaign headquarters. Under President Reagan, Ed Rollins and Lee Atwater were the first to begin planning for 1984 and the first to leave the White House for the reelection campaign. During the Clinton administration, Political Director Douglas Sosnick played a highly visible and influential role in campaign planning, and, unlike his predecessors, he remained in the White House. The Bush reelection campaign was unique in that while an Office of Political Affairs existed, it was not utilized for early campaign planning since President Bush selected his most senior campaign aides from outside the White House.

A second trend related to reelection campaigns is the increasing involvement of outside advisers. Ever since President Ford's reelection campaign in 1976, presidents have turned to private-sector political consultants. In many cases, these "outsiders" are veteran campaign strategists who wield a great deal of influence—Stu Spencer, Pat Caddell, Bob Teeter, Fred Malek and Richard Morris. So while the White House plays the lead role in reelection campaigns, as election day nears, the inner circle often expands to include outside political consultants.

For Presidents Eisenhower through Ford, it is more difficult to generalize about the location from which initial campaign operatives emerged, in part because the Office of Political Affairs did not exist. More importantly, the overall size and structure of the White House has changed so dramatically in the past forty years that it is nearly impossible to generalize. Furthermore, the brevity of the Ford term, the circumstances under which Johnson assumed office and the uncertainty surrounding the 1956 and 1968 decisions to seek reelection complicate efforts to generalize.

Though it is difficult to provide a concise response to the question of who participates in the president's campaign, these days one can look to the Office of Political Affairs, the chief of staff and senior presidential aides—all are common participants in early reelection planning. One can also generalize by saying that among those participating in early planning efforts, many staff members were involved in the previous campaign in some capacity; they may have directed the president's statewide campaign or been a senior strategist. It is likely that this initial experience accounts for their involvement in the president's reelection campaign.

WHEN DO PRESIDENTS BEGIN LONG-TERM REELECTION PLANNING?[9]

Identifying when presidents begin planning for reelection requires the discovery of a consistent benchmark. For example, Harry Dent, a Nixon aide, wrote, "The 1972 campaign for reelection of the president of the United States was underway from the time the Nixon team entered the White House in January 1969."[10] When members of the Carter White House staff were asked when they began gearing up for the reelection campaign, some jokingly stated, "November 1976." After this response, they admitted that, in fact, they were too caught up in the "daily grind" to think about such a distant event. However, they were aware that every task they performed was done to cast the president in the best light, and to some, this was equivalent to planning for 1980.[11]

Since it is often difficult to distinguish between campaign planning and performing a job that is inherently political, this book defines campaign planning as a series of concrete efforts conducted strictly and solely for the forthcoming election. Such early efforts typically include strategic campaign planning and the recruiting of campaign personnel. These early planning efforts are important elements of the overall campaign because they lay the foundation of what will eventually become a nationwide campaign. In a book by a former White House staff member, the importance of early planning is stated by Nixon Chief of Staff H.R. Haldeman to aide Jeb Magruder, "'You've got a great opportunity to build a campaign from the ground up. This is the most important thing we'll be doing in the next two years.'"[12]

A fair reading of presidential campaign history indicates that presidents typically begin gearing up for reelection after the midterm elections. "[It] is important to point out that the conclusion of a midterm election almost immediately focuses attention on the next presidential election."[13] According to a *National Journal* article written during President Carter's tenure:

> With the midterm elections over, movement in the designated areas
> will be intensified in preparation for the second half of President

Carter's term, as well as with an eye toward the 1980 presidential campaign and a second term in office.[14]

Presidents frequently campaign on behalf of members of Congress and tend to see the midterm election as the first popular evaluation of their tenure. Since the president's party usually loses seats in midterm elections, the poor performance provides the impetus to the staff and the president to begin thinking about the forthcoming campaign.

There are essentially two ways of documenting the start of campaign planning: one is by examining candidate records filed at the Federal Election Commission (FEC) and the second is by relying on presidential documents, secondary sources and information obtained in personal interviews. After 1974, presidential candidates were required to file a formal statement of candidacy with the FEC. The formal declaration is often filed at the point the campaign begins to raise money,

An individual becomes a candidate for Federal office (and thus triggers registration and reporting obligations under the Act) when his or her campaign exceeds $5,000 in either contributions or expenditures.[15]

Set out below are the dates when presidents filed this formal statement.

When Incumbent Presidential Campaign Filed with FEC

Campaign	Months before Election	Statement of Candidacy Filing Date[16]
Ford 1976	17	6/75
Carter 1980	20	3/79
Reagan 1984	13	10/83
Bush 1992	13	10/91
Clinton 1996	19	4/95

Note, however, that this date is not the earliest indication of campaign planning because planning can and does occur before the formal declaration of candidacy. Nonetheless, it is the earliest publicly documented indicator of campaign planning and has a rough sense of accuracy.

Set out below is another set of dates that represents when informal campaign planning began.

When Reelection Campaign Planning Begins

Campaign	Months before Election	Date
Eisenhower 1956	21	2/55
Johnson 1964	11	12/63
Johnson	12	11/67
Nixon	24	11/70
Ford	18	5/75
Carter	24	11/78
Reagan	34	1/82
Bush	15	8/91
Clinton	24	11/94

Presidents Nixon, Carter, Reagan and Clinton began planning for the reelection campaign in the same year as the midterm election, while Presidents Eisenhower, Johnson, Ford and Bush started planning in the third year of the term. Note, however, that the Johnson '64 and Ford campaigns could not have started much sooner than they did given the special circumstances surrounding their ascension to the presidency.

Eisenhower's ambivalence about seeking reelection did not deter his staff and the RNC from planning his campaign. The earliest recorded effort of reelection planning for 1956 occurs in February of 1955 when Eisenhower's appointments secretary moved to New York to set up a campaign headquarters.[17] Despite the unfortunate circumstances leading up to LBJ's campaign in 1964, an examination of this campaign illustrates that delayed planning is a common theme in both the 1964 and 1968 presidential campaigns. Ambivalence alone in 1968 did not fully account for the delayed campaign preparation. Consider Johnson's behavior in the 1964 campaign:

> Johnson had not even named a campaign manager by the time the convention rolled around . . . His campaign organization—disorganization was the better word—defied schematic description . . . He ended up with no campaign manager at all, except Lyndon Johnson.[18]

Johnson's indecision in 1968 may have postponed planning, but his performance in 1964 indicates that preplanning and organization were not prominent features of his presidential campaigns.

In regard to long-term planning, Johnson's 1968 campaign is unique in that planning efforts were stalled, reflecting his long-standing ambivalence toward seeking reelection. President Johnson's announcement in March of 1968 that he would not seek reelection helps explain why there was an absence of long-term planning. Formal strategy sessions did not occur until November of 1967, just three months before the first primary. While planning efforts exist, they began much later than in other administrations.

There are two basic schools of thought concerning the delayed planning for the 1968 election. One school asserts that Johnson had been planning his withdrawal from the race for months, but was waiting for the opportune moment to announce his resignation. The other school of thought is that the President's poor performance in early primaries, the state of the economy, the onslaught of student uprisings and his depiction as the "war candidate" forced him to consider withdrawal. The only thing that is clear is that nobody knows for sure, not even close aides. Speechwriter Harry McPherson still contends that the decision surrounding Johnson's candidacy (or lack thereof) in 1968 was "really a puzzler." In fact, Mr. McPherson recounted a story in which he recently ran into a White House colleague at the grocery store who, twenty-four years later, still wanted to know why Johnson decided not to run. McPherson replied that the precise reason for his withdrawal remained a mystery.[19]

President Nixon and his team began preparation shortly after the midterm elections. Initial strategy meetings began November 7, 1970, just four days after the midterm elections. Among those in attendance were President Nixon, John Mitchell, H.R. Haldeman, John Ehrlichman, Robert Finch, Charles Colson, Donald Rumsfeld and Bryce Harlow.[20] "Subject number one was the campaign of 1972—which meant a look at the results of the 1970 election just over and what they told of the future."[21] Subsequently, the White House established a task force to plan the reelection campaign, and by midspring of 1971, the campaign operation opened up across the street from the White House. This relatively early start can be explained by Nixon's plummeting ratings, the congressional losses at the midterm and fear of a tough Democratic challenge. According to Jeb Magruder, an early White House aide-turned-campaign-staff member, "We felt that it was going to be a very difficult race. . . . So we were concerned and we started early for that reason."[22]

The Ford administration began thinking about reelection shortly after assuming office in August of 1974, though actual planning did not begin for several months:

> On the Republican side, Ford had begun to think about and position himself for a term in his own right almost immediately after his succession, and he had spent much of his abbreviated tenure in the White House trying first to discourage Ronald Reagan from challenging him for the GOP nomination and then beating back that challenge.[23]

His odd succession into office made him the first wholly unelected president—he was neither elected to the vice presidency nor the presidency. Thus, Ford had no electoral base to expand upon nor did he have any experience running a nationwide campaign. These unique circumstances necessitated intense campaign preparation that began in May of 1975.

In the case of the Carter administration, strategic planning began in the late fall of 1978. According to journalist Elizabeth Drew:

> Among those at the meetings were Hamilton Jordan, then the
> President's top assistant and now his chief of staff; Jody Powell, the
> President's press secretary; Caddell [the President's pollster]; Kraft
> and Gerald Rafshoon, the President's media adviser. They arrived at a
> four-part strategy: start early; anticipate the toughest possible
> opposition; run everywhere; and spend carefully.[24]

In February of 1979 Tim Kraft began to lay the foundation for the
Carter/Mondale Campaign Committee by setting up field organizations
in key states.[25] By the summer of 1979, six major trade unions
endorsed the president.[26] These early organizational efforts and public
declarations of support were no doubt an attempt to demonstrate
President Carter's impenetrability while dissuading fellow Democrats
like Kennedy from challenging the President.

Prior to the midterm elections in 1982, Ed Rollins and Lee
Atwater, from the Office of Political Affairs, stepped in to begin
preparations for Reagan's reelection campaign in 1984. According to
Ed Rollins, "When I took over as director of the White House political
office in January 1982 . . . Lee Atwater, who was my deputy, and I
decided we would focus for that year on the West and the South, which
we thought were very, very crucial to putting together the necessary
electoral votes."[27] In June of 1983, Lee Atwater took a swing through
the south in order to formulate a southern campaign strategy: "I
remember very distinctly in June of 1983 I went to five southern states
in the course of the month and came back and met with Ed Rollins, Bob
Teeter, Roger Stone and others, and we decided several things."[28] By
October of 1983, Atwater, Rollins and the rest of the Office of Political
Affairs left the White House and moved to the Reagan/Bush campaign
headquarters. Upon their departure, James Baker's personal aide,
Margaret Tutwiler, assumed the helm at the Office of Political Affairs
and served as the White House liaison to the campaign.

President Reagan himself initiated an early form of reelection
planning when, on election day in 1982, he asked Paul Laxalt to be
general chairman of the Republican party:

> He [Reagan] was quite plainly beginning to arrange the furniture for
> 1984, and he asked Laxalt to accept an undefined position as 'general
> chairman' of the party.[29]

This method of appointing a well-known Republican senator as general
chair was not repeated by Reagan's successors until President Clinton
in January of 1995 appointed a well-known Democratic Senator,
Christopher Dodd, as general chair of the Democratic National
Committee.[30] At any rate, shortly after Reagan's appointment of
Senator Laxalt, two White House insiders, Baker and Deaver, and two
outsiders, veteran strategist Stuart Spencer and presidential pollster,
Bob Teeter began holding secret planning meetings. The same group
had been meeting regularly since 1981, albeit without focusing on the
1984 election.[31]

Campaign planning for President Bush began much later than the
Reagan and Carter administrations. Though it is not clear why there
was a delay in early planning efforts, observers speculate that Bush's
historically high approval ratings in the wake of the Operation Desert
Storm victory created an air of confidence that postponed campaign
planning. Several months prior to the establishment of his campaign
committee and thus his first formal filing with the FEC, President Bush
was riding high in the polls. The aftermath of Operation Desert Storm
cast a glow around the White House and the citizenry awarded the
President the highest approval ratings in polling history. In March of
1991, a point at which some previous presidents' reelection campaigns
were well underway, President Bush's job performance, calculated by
Gallup, was as high as 90%.[32] At the same time, potential Democratic
challengers were publicly declaring their noncandidacy, primarily
citing the "needs of their family" as the major reason for sitting out the
election. President Bush was basking in the glow of a military victory
with no challenger in sight, and thus no reason to start the engines of
his reelection vehicle.

According to Bush/Quayle Political Director Mary Matalin, an
initial strategy was formulated in August of 1991. "It [the campaign
strategy] was long-lived, and it actually was laid out, sketched out with
some definition at Camp David in August of 1991, and we did

repeatedly try to come back to it."[33] However, no campaign structure per se had been established in August 1991. One month later, *The Washington Post* reported, "If President Bush has made up his mind for a campaign structure and timing, it is still a mystery to many of those who expect to play key roles in the campaign."[34] Shortly thereafter, the economic picture began to look dimmer and the President's ratings steadily declined. The result was predictable, "President Bush, thrown on the defensive by continued economic problems and Democratic criticism, plans to try to regain political momentum by accelerating the formation of his official reelection campaign, according to a senior administration official."[35] Bush initially appointed three campaign veterans to head up his reelection campaign. These campaign leaders, all non–White House staff, included campaign veteran and pollster Robert Teeter, former Nixon assistant Fred Malek and former Secretary of Commerce Robert Mosbacher. A new chief of staff, Samuel Skinner, replaced John Sununu at roughly the same time.

President Clinton, perhaps in an all-out effort to avoid the missteps of the Bush reelection campaign, began planning his reelection campaign after the disastrous midterm elections in 1994. In order to prepare for this critical event, weekly strategy meetings were held in the White House residence and included the President, the Vice President, his chief of staff, senior White House staff members (chief of staff, deputy chiefs of staff, press secretary, political director, senior adviser, chief speechwriter, First Lady's chief of staff, deputy national security adviser, presidential counselor), Clinton/Gore campaign staff (campaign manager and deputy manager), select Cabinet members (Cisneros, Housing and Urban Development and Kantor, Commerce) outside consultants (Richard Morris, Robert Squier, Bill Knapp), pollster (Mark Penn), and the chair of the Democratic Party. While one can confidently speculate about the topic of conversation, one account explicitly indicated that:

> At these sessions, Mr Clinton and his advisers always pore over poll results from the week before; fiddle with their new television commercials, but also, on a broader level, exchange ideas about the

Presidents's message of the week and how best to counter Bob Dole, the presumed Republican nominee. [36]

Faced with an immediate vacancy in the DNC chair's office in December of 1994, the first priority of the White House was to fill that position. According to one report:

> The DNC chairmanship is the first of several major personnel decisions Clinton must make as he looks ahead to a difficult reelection campaign ... White House officials are not anxious to plunge into reelection politics, but given the Republican resurgence, Clinton's unpopularity and talk about a primary challenge to Clinton among nervous Democrats, they are aware they will have to move more rapidly than George Bush did four years ago. [37]

After the midterm elections, Deputy Chief of Staff Harold Ickes began campaign planning in earnest, focusing primarily on important reelection-related personnel decisions, while other participants set their sights on the big picture.

Though it is possible to identify a general time period during which initial campaign planning begins, such planning does not incite a marked change in White House operations. According to Nixon aide, John Ehrlichman, "How can you say when a campaign begins? There's no sharp demarcation line, you just glide into it. . . . The campaign of 1972 began just after the campaign of 1970, some time in 1971 when we were thinking about the State-of-the-Union Message for 1972." [38] This sentiment about the absence of "demarcation lines" and "gliding" into planning is commonplace among former Carter and Reagan staff members as well. A Carter staff member expressed a similar attitude: "The campaign is always in the back of your mind because it is a fixed date on the calendar that gets nearer and nearer. You don't all of the sudden say ok, it's time to start thinking about reelection, it's 1980." [39] It is also important to note that though planning begins after midterm elections, the effort is not as formalized a process as the preceding description may at times suggest. Many times campaign planning may occur inadvertently in a brief hallway conversation, rather than in a systematic fashion.

Another important point about long-term campaign planning is that the president plays a minimal role in these early efforts. Instead, his closest advisers strategize and prepare for the forthcoming election. "You have to remember that we had a White House political office which basically started a campaign two years before the President [Reagan] did."[40] Understandably, the president does not participate in the earliest form of campaign planning that typically involves nuts-and-bolts planning and logistics. A select group of White House staff members, with the oversight of the chief of staff, can handle these efforts without the president, and the president probably prefers to remain on the periphery, devoting his attention to other presidential duties and issues.

WHAT TYPES OF CAMPAIGN PLANNING ACTIVITIES OCCUR?

The following section identifies and explains long- and short-term campaign planning activities originating in the White House. Prior to the formal establishment of a campaign operation, those participating in the early reelection planning activities focus on two major activities: recruitment and strategic planning. These long-term planning efforts form the foundation of the president's national campaign organization. Though campaigning has changed substantially since the Eisenhower era, one staple is the central role of the White House in short-term campaign planning. Once election year arrives, members of the White House participate in strategy formulation, establish a liaison mechanism between the campaign organization and the White House, and actively campaign throughout the country.

Long-term Reelection Planning Activities

Constructing a campaign team is perhaps the first and most important long-term planning activity. Those involved in recruitment focus on three sources: White House staff members who are experienced campaigners, campaign veterans in the private sector who participated in the previous presidential campaign and staff members from the party organization.

Assembling a national field organization is particularly important if there is a primary challenge. In a 1978 memo from Hamilton Jordan to President Carter, Jordan indicated the pressing need to be organized for the primary season:

> Caucuses and primaries will begin in fifteen months. Some organizational work will have to be done in early 1979. What is the best way to reconcile the need on one hand to be well organized with the corresponding need not to appear to be preoccupied with reelection?[41]

Many times veteran campaigners who organized a state in the previous campaign will return, reestablish their political connections and set up the president's campaign operation in the same state.

In terms of strategy formulation, participants consider the president's record in the White House, the development of a future policy agenda, the interpretation of polling data, the assessment of possible primary challengers and general election opponents, and the development of themes and messages. According to Republican campaign veteran Stuart Spencer, in the Ford and Reagan reelection campaigns the staff spent ample time reviewing the president's policy record and anticipating future policy.[42] "They [White House officials] are taking a hard look at demographic trends, undoubtedly with a mind toward tailoring the President's 1984 campaign promises to appeal to a broad range of voters throughout the nation."[43] Ed Meese, the counselor to President Reagan, directed a group that studied future policy options and campaign themes.

Similarly, in the Bush administration, efforts were made to develop an agenda which would provide the electorate with an indicator of what the next four years would entail.

That is why the President has instructed his staff to focus on defining
a broad agenda for the next five years, the officials say—an order that
came as Mr. Bush shifted his attention to the general election and
away from a primary season that had been much meaner than any of
his advisers had predicted.[44]

Citizens need to know why they should cast their vote for the president
and, in order to make this decision, the president must provide them
with a blueprint for the future. The Clinton administration followed
such a strategy by utilizing election-year commencement addresses to
outline his foreign, economic and social policies, all in an effort ". . . to
answer critics who say he still has not painted a full vision for a second
term."[45] Thus, in preparation for the election the White House must not
only carefully scrutinize its current record, but articulate an agenda for
the forthcoming term.

Another strategic concern is the electoral college, a unique feature
of American presidential elections, which has a profound impact on
campaign strategy.

. . . the present method of electing the president tends to give greater
power to the large, populous states, not the small, empty states,
because the large states can deliver to the winner large blocs of the
votes he needs to win. Consequently, presidential nominees tend to
come from big states and tend to run on platforms likely to appeal to
interest groups that cluster there. They concentrate their campaigns in
the big population centers and, as politicians know, they stand or fall
on the big state votes.[46]

Strategists closely monitor state-by-state support, as reflected in public
opinion polls, so that they can allocate resources in a way that will
facilitate the assembly of a winning coalition of states. Those states
with low levels of presidential support and a significant number of
electoral votes are prime targets for resource allocation.

Conversely, presidents are unlikely to allocate time and other
resources to "safe" states, regardless of a potentially large share of
electoral votes. One recent example illustrating this strategy concerns

the airing of television commercials: "Paid for by the Democratic National Committee, the campaign has largely sidestepped the Northeast and stayed out of big cities like New York, Los Angeles and San Francisco, where Mr. Clinton is considered safely ahead and television time is expensive."[47] Given a finite amount of money to spend during the general election, presidents must carefully allocate their resources—what this entails is a series of calculated decisions concerning which states are capable of providing the president with a plurality of votes and whether the state possesses a significant number of electoral votes. The electoral college math requires presidents to monitor their state-by-state support as well as their overall electoral coalition.

Campaign fundraising is another key element of long-term strategy. While the president and his staff cannot legally conduct fundraising efforts from the White House, they can strategize about how and when to begin this all important effort. The Clinton administration set all-time records by raising $26.5 million in 1995, an entire year before the election.[48] Such aggressive fundraising was part of an overall strategy to fend off potential primary challengers. Since fundraising is the fuel that enables the campaign to function, early efforts are key to the success of the campaign. In addition, during the post–Federal Election Campaign Act (FECA) era, there is a strong incentive for campaigns to raise money during the nomination season because such funds will be matched (the federal government will match individual campaign contributions of $250 or less received by candidates who raised $5,000 in twenty states)[49], thereby adding a significant bonus amount to the campaign coffers. Candidates are able to collect matching contributions as early as January 1 of the year preceding the election year. Given the legal environment of modern campaigning, early fundraising efforts are an essential component for the establishment of a strong financial base and ultimately a strong campaign. According to a campaign strategy memo by Lee Atwater, the federal funding enabled the Reagan campaign to develop a strong campaign operation:

This [the absence of a primary challenger] gives our campaign the opportunity to use our allotted $21.5 million—and these ten months—to build a strong organization. If we put the money into voter registration, local organizing and some spot media, we can secure our electoral base earlier than any campaign in history.[50]

Another example of long-term planning is more subtle, but nevertheless brings benefit to the president's campaign, and that is the president's ability to have several White House staff members performing quasi-governmental tasks that may lend themselves to garnering public support:

Not the least of his assets is a loyal White House staff that, in the unavoidable blurring of presidential and political functions, performs a myriad of services for him and hence his candidacy.[51]

These services, of course, vary across presidencies, but typically include efforts to nourish relationships with key constituencies and elected officials. Various White House offices like Political Affairs, Intergovernmental Affairs, Public Liaison and Congressional Relations perform tasks that produce tangible political benefits. For example, nurturing relationships with mayors, governors, key constituencies and Members of Congress over a four-year period can prove to be beneficial when the president's campaign needs assistance or endorsements. In the Carter White House, Jack Watson, presidential Assistant for Intergovernmental Affairs, was largely responsible for harnessing support from elected officials.[52] Such efforts to maintain or expand public support are not uncommon. An example from the Reagan administration demonstrates White House efforts to galvanize public support:

By the end of April [1981], [Elizabeth] Dole's office [Public Liaison] had engineered 19 meetings at which the president or vice president spoke, 89 White House sessions with Cabinet and staff members, 148 follow-up talks and nine large-scale East Room briefings. Dole's outside speaking engagements numbered 29. She collected general endorsements of the economic program from nearly 200 groups and corporations.[53]

Though these tasks, coalition-building and outreach, are part of everyday business and are perfectly legitimate aspects of the governing process, it is nonetheless true that successful performance of these tasks also helps insure that when election year rolls around, the support and endorsements roll in as well. Those constituencies invited to the White House to attend a briefing or those mayors who were recipients of generous grants will not be reluctant to support the president in his second bid for the presidency. Admittedly these offices cannot please everyone. The game of politics always involves winners and losers. But, in the end, the support lost by staff efforts will be outweighed by gaining substantial support from other areas.

In addition to the White House staff galvanizing support, staff members also provide advice and information. For example,

Ford has at his fingertips a team of experts in every field of government to develop positions for him, and none of the work is charged against the President's campaign funds.[54]

Policy analysts are paid to study policy alternatives and there is nothing illegal about exploiting these avenues of advice in an election year. During the 1996 election season, the Clinton White House was noted for its prompt and thorough opposition research and the related ability to respond expeditiously to the opponent's negative advertising or other verbal barbs. "The White House has become relentless in its opposition research, answering Senator Bob Dole's call for a repeal of the 4.3-cent-a-gallon tax on gasoline with a list of gasoline tax increases that the Senator supported."[55] Such staff resources are an incredibly valuable asset to the president's campaign and it is difficult to label such activities as overtly political when they occur in the course of daily White House business.

Short-term Reelection Planning Activities

In the short term, strategy formulation focuses on analyzing and criticizing the opposition's record as well as the White House record, considering future policy initiatives, conducting polling analysis and developing themes. Strategists are constantly reviewing polling data, assessing it and revising the state-by-state strategy. Along with these efforts, schedulers must determine the best use of the president's time—where and how to spend it (e.g., pancake breakfasts, rallies, commencement addresses).

Theme Development and Agenda-setting

Developing a campaign theme is at once the most difficult and important task of the campaign. A campaign memorandum from Ford strategists demonstrates the importance of theme development:

> The President, the Administration and the campaign need a *theme*. I am concerned that the President is seen as a tactician without an overall strategy of his plan for the country. This lets voters and his opponents interpret many of his perceptions and programs as those done for political expedience or to appease special interest groups rather than as part of an overall plan to move the country toward a perceived set of goals or objectives. We need an umbrella under which we can put all of the President's programs and end up with the whole being greater than the sum of its parts.[56]

In the 1980 election, Carter and his strategists were forever searching for an appealing campaign theme. Ronald Reagan's 1984 campaign theme, "It's morning again in America," captured the hearts of many voters. The Bush campaign in 1992, on the other hand, was constantly criticized for its lack of a unifying theme. And in 1996, President Clinton repeatedly hammered home his ability to "build a bridge to the twenty-first century." Once the campaign decides on a theme, it may be cast aside later if found to be ineffective, but after a successful theme has been developed, the president's team has a distinct advantage over the challenger.

This advantage stems largely from the incumbent's ability to control the political agenda:

> The President can say in the morning, 'I want to say this today,' the speechwriters can work on it, advance notice can be given to the press, the press can be briefed, and the President can say it at four-o'clock—in time to get on the air.[57]

Because of the president's visibility in the media, the White House has the ability to set the agenda by determining what aspects of the president's activities the press will cover. A member of the Carter White House staff indicated that during the campaign they held morning meetings to discuss how they could affect the content of the evening news. Their strategy was not to let the president in front of the camera except for the one event that they wanted the press to cover. This staff member emphasized that it was important to control the content as much as possible.[58] In the age of media-dominated campaigns, White House agenda-setting is key; the president's campaign must be able to force the opponent to react to their agenda, not vice versa. The appearance and reality of control is extremely beneficial to the success of an incumbent's campaign operation.

Another means of campaign agenda-setting is to involve the president in a specific type of event. For instance, if the White House wanted to raise the issue of housing for the homeless, the scheduling office could arrange for the president to visit housing sites that have been created as a result of current administration policy. An example of this strategy was put forth by the Bush administration during the election year. Since foreign policy was deemed to be President Bush's forte, the administration thought that focusing on this issue would play to Bush's skills and against his opponent's (Bill Clinton):

> The White House is counting on a series of foreign trips and diplomatic events in coming months to resurrect foreign policy as a campaign issue and reassert President Bush's primacy in world affairs before the fall election . . . For Mr. Bush and his political

advisers, the effort is in part an attempt to redirect the political debate . . . [59]

By allowing Bush to demonstrate his skills as chief diplomat, the question of foreign policy leadership was then turned to the opponent, who was thought to have great difficulty demonstrating expertise or experience in foreign affairs.

Playing the foreign policy card is not a new strategy. In 1972, Nixon made a diplomatic trip to China which was thought to be politically motivated. During this trip, he managed to sign an arms limitation treaty with the Soviet Union and finalize negotiations ending the Vietnam conflict. The Democratic candidate, George McGovern, was struggling to gain support against a competitor who was cast as a world leader for all the country to see. In short, the president's ability to set the agenda is an extremely valuable asset as is the related ability to strategically time such events.

The Rose Garden Strategy

Apart from setting the agenda, presidents seek to maintain the presidential aura while campaigning for reelection. They do so by adopting the "Rose Garden strategy," a common short-term campaign strategy utilized by presidents in an effort to remain above the campaign fray. Presidents from Eisenhower through Clinton have considered the pros and cons of the Rose Garden strategy and many have adopted it for various lengths of time over the course of the campaign. The desire to remain "presidential" is even greater for those facing a tough primary challenge. President Ford faced a difficult primary challenge and was advised to take the "high ground," appear as a leader and avoid looking like a candidate. "Ford's strategist . . . had no intention of permitting the incumbent President to race around the countryside like a candidate for assemblyman."[60] Despite this declared *modus operandi*, President Ford campaigned extensively, "Ford already has visited 42 states. . . . From the beginning of 1975 through his trip November 2, [1975], Ford spent 86 out of 306 days traveling outside Washington."[61] Ford ultimately was advised to cut down on travel because his ratings were dropping. A campaign strategy memo written roughly three months before the Iowa caucus cautioned:

> Even though he [Ford] is a candidate and will be engaged in a political campaign all next year, he ought to remain as non-political and as far from the battle as possible. Every time he gives a hard, strident political speech, he hurts his strongest point, and that is his perception as being honest, candid and fair.[62]

According to Stuart Spencer, "Ford did better when he was in the White House, so the Rose Garden strategy suited him perfectly."[63] Most presidents prefer to remain in the White House with all the trappings and prestige that the position bestows on them rather than becoming involved in the partisan battles that pervade the campaign arena.

After fifty American hostages were held hostage in Tehran, Iran in November of 1979, President Carter announced that he was unable to campaign given the gravity of the situation. He asserted that his first priority was governing and, more precisely, bringing the hostages safely home.[64] Though Carter adopted this strategy shortly after his formal announcement that he would seek reelection in December of 1979, he abandoned it roughly five months later (early May) when the race against Democratic Senator Edward Kennedy heated up and presidential approval ratings declined. He then shed the low-profile campaign image for a more interactive campaign strategy. According to one observer:

> President Carter's explanation for ending his self-imposed Rose Garden exile and beginning active campaigning for reelection may rank as one of the most nakedly deceptive acts of his Administration.[65]

Nonetheless, the Reagan campaign feared an "October Surprise," in which the hostages would return just before election day. President Carter's attempts to free the hostages failed and they did not return home until months after the election in January of 1980. It was apparent that Carter sought to use the Rose Garden strategy for electoral gain and when it proved itself a hindrance, he cast it aside.

Presidents also tend to adopt this Rose Garden strategy even when no primary challenge exists. Political consultants and presidential confidants agree that it is better for the president to appear presidential than as a candidate begging for support. Once the primary challenge of Patrick Buchanan dissipated, White House and campaign strategists promoted a Rose Garden strategy for President Bush. Though he maintained this appearance, he of course did not refrain entirely from campaigning:

> The 'Rose Garden strategy' of getting President Bush off the campaign trail and back in the White House to demonstrate Presidential leadership was not intended to cut down on the number of visitors to the White House. Yesterday, Mr. Bush gave a basketball exhibition in a decidedly soccer fashion to Digger Phelps, former Notre Dame coach, and members of the McDonald's high school all-star team.[66]

Adhering in a different way to the Rose Garden strategy, President Clinton deliberately refrained from formally announcing his candidacy, though such a ploy did not prevent observers and opponents from declaring that the White House was in campaign mode.

The critical factor dictating the use of the Rose Garden strategy is whether the president can improve his support by campaigning. If not, the president remains in the White House and adopts a Rose Garden strategy. If his ratings increase while he is campaigning across the country, then it is unlikely that consultants will suggest that the president adopt a Rose Garden strategy. It goes without saying that adoption of the Rose Garden strategy is not done for the good of the country or the government, as many presidents would like voters to think; rather it is adopted because it is thought to be best for the president's reelection prospects. Furthermore, no president ever completely refrains from campaigning when he remains in the White House. The President, First Lady and Vice President will often make numerous phone calls to supporters and potential supporters. In addition, during an election year, the White House receives many visitors under the guise of a policy briefing or reception.

White House as Campaign Tool

Making use of the White House by inviting voters to various events is thought to be a highly effective means of gaining support. A White House memorandum from H.R. Haldeman demonstrates the importance of these efforts:

> Since we are now entering a political year, the value of White House invitations, from a political standpoint, obviously has increased over what they already are. Would it therefore be possible for me to start reviewing all the invitation lists to White House events for political reasons, prior to the time they are forwarded to the Social Office to be sent out?[67]

Another example of campaign-motivated White House entertaining was provided by a Carter staff member who indicated that roughly six weeks before a primary or caucus they would host what they called a "State Day" in which the White House invited roughly 400 state Democrats (residents of the state holding the forthcoming primary contest), elected officials, committee people and Carter supporters. These guests would be briefed by senior staff members, receive a tour of the White House and an afternoon drink and snack. President and Mrs. Carter would circulate through the crowd and then the President would speak to the group. The day would end with a photo opportunity with the President and First Lady. These efforts were thought to be a successful means of maintaining, and possibly expanding political support.[68]

The Clinton administration added new meaning to the phrase "White House as campaign tool" by allowing some donors the chance to sleep in the Lincoln bedroom, attend a state dinner or a briefing in the Map Room. Biweekly coffees, once thought to be a major perk, were modest events in comparison to the experiences for select donors during the Clinton administration. According to one news report, ". . . this year Mr. Clinton relentlessly used all the perks and power of incumbency to raise money. . . . Mr. Clinton and Mr. Gore presided over unpublicized, small gatherings aimed at rewarding the largest donors with access to the highest echelons of power."[69]

Liaison with Reelection Committee

A common facet of all presidential reelection campaigns is the development of a liaison between the White House and the campaign organization. According to Reagan campaign liaison Margaret Tutwiler:

> You have two massive organizations. I didn't have everything come through me. That would be ridiculous because the campaign creates a press organization, a public liaison organization, a governors' organization, etc. It mirrors basically the White House organization. It's not intentional; it's just that all campaigns have those sections in order to implement the political tasks that need to be done and can only appropriately be done from a political organization.[70]

Given the parallel nature of the White House and the campaign apparatus, a coordinator is integral to their proper functioning. "The effective integration of the Government (particularly the White House) and the campaign can be decisive. We cannot hope to maximize our advantages if they simply overlap—they must be integrated."[71] This liaison is usually a White House staff member who spends substantial time communicating with the campaign organization. This sharing and comparing of information is often then conveyed to White House strategists. The liaison also acts as a contact point at the White House when problems or questions arise and therefore he or she takes on a great deal of administrative work. Designating a liaison is thought to add a degree of coherence to the president's campaign message as well as critical coordination between the two groups' efforts. And, not surprisingly, there tends to be a fair amount of friction between those on the front line of battle at the campaign headquarters and the "decisionmakers" in the White House.

From the Nixon administration:

> I continue to see evidence that the Committee for the Reelection Staff and the White House staff are meshing very badly on matters of substantive policy and how to use it politically . . . Committee staff can't seem to stay away from calling everyone in the government to ask for information on substantive programs and policy. Departments, agencies, OMB, my staff all are getting calls from new people, just on the scene, determined to reinvent the wheels which long ago have been thoroughly invented. Moreover, they tactlessly seek to exploit "non-political" efforts in the clumsier kind of way. [72]

From the Carter administration:

> I am sending to Hamilton a memorandum that outlines in greater detail the specific needs of the Campaign Committee in relationship to the White House . . . There is a serious morale problem at the Committee and one of its causes is a feeling of 'apartness' from you and the White House . . . The basic point is that I can't 'leave' politics here [the White House] with Sarah [Weddington] while I go over to 'organize' the campaign. [73]

From the Bush campaign:

> But the most frustrating, miserable, teeth-gnashing problem for a reelection campaign is weaving into the existing governmental structure. It wasn't personal, we pretty much all liked each other, and everybody, of course, loved George Bush—but the people at the White House thought the campaign people were dopes, Neanderthals and thugs. [74]

The Bush administration adopted a liaison mechanism called the "funnel" in which a small number of White House staff members were designated as campaign contacts. That is, these staff members were the only ones permitted to be in direct contact with the campaign. If anyone from the campaign needed information from the White House or the executive branch, they were instructed to work through the "funnel." The idea was largely the product of White House Counsel Boyden Gray who was concerned about the ethical issue of separating campaign business from official business. According to Bush/Quayle political director Mary Matalin:

> To speak to the speechwriter or anyone at the White House, in every single instance I'd have to write a memo, go to Teeter, explain what we needed and why we needed to speak directly. Teeter would have to go to Skinner, Skinner would have to go to Boyden. Boyden would have to consider it, give the permission, get back to Skinner, who'd get back to Teeter or Malek, who would get back to me. By that time we'd given the speech, minus the local input.[75]

Not surprisingly, this mechanism proved to be inoperable and was discarded shortly after its adoption.[76]

In addition to the creation of a liaison mechanism, the White House senior staff and the campaign meet frequently to discuss the president's schedule, activities, events and possible strategies. During the Ford and Reagan reelection campaigns, a group consisting of White House and campaign staff met every morning at 7:00 a.m. to discuss the campaign. Veteran campaigner Stuart Spencer pointed out that what was important about this group of "insiders" and "outsiders" was the chemistry—that the group be able to discuss and end up with an agreement and that there be full usage of assets available to the president both inside and outside the White House.[77] He also noted that the success of the group meetings in 1976 led to their adoption in 1984.

Staff Campaigning

In the nomination stage of the campaign, strategic participation is concentrated among senior staff members: the chief of staff, scheduler, pollster, special assistants and counselors to the president. The domestic policy adviser and other specialists occasionally participate in strategy sessions. Other members of the senior staff participate by acting as presidential surrogates in regions where support is weak. And some staff members participate by volunteering their weekends and vacation time to campaign for the president. Though most of the president's staff remain in the White House during an election year, several members actually resign their White House positions to join the campaign staff. Alternatively, members of the Carter administration recalled days in which they would put in the requisite eight hours at the White House and then another eight hours of unpaid labor at the campaign headquarters. Additionally, many of these staff members took leaves of absence or used vacation time to campaign in Iowa, New Hampshire or other key primary states.

It is important to note that White House staff members cannot substitute government work with campaign–related work; campaigning must be done on one's free time. According to a Carter White House memorandum outlining political activity guidelines,

> White House staff members must perform their official duties for 40 hours per week or 80 hours per two week period. They are presumed to be on their own time before 9:00 a.m. and after 5:30 p.m., Monday through Friday and all day Saturday, Sunday and legal holidays . . . It may be necessary to allocate or pro-rate between the government and the campaign the salaries of White House staff members who spent significant, discrete blocks of time, during the regular work day, on campaign activities. [78]

Another memorandum emphatically states,

> White House facilities and personnel will continue to be used solely for governmental purposes. Federal resources may not be used for anything but official purposes. This means that *all* campaign costs must be paid from campaign funds. [79]

In 1992, there were similar efforts to put a cap on campaign involvement. Prior to Mr. Baker's resignation as Secretary of State and assumption of the chief of staff position, the counsel to the President issued a relevant memorandum:

> Mr. Bush's old friend and counsel, C. Boyden Gray, had only recently issued a memorandum arguing that, from an ethical point of

view, campaign tasks should not be undertaken by members of the
White House staff, which of course is what Mr. Baker plans to do.[80]

The White House spokesman, Marlin Fitzwater, responded to relevant
ethical questions by stating that politics and policy were inseparable;
thereby attempting to legitimize Mr. Baker's campaign activities as
White House chief of staff.

Despite the fact that the legal counsel to two Presidents—from
different political parties no less—has each concluded that campaign
activity may not be pursued on official time, it is not clear to what
degree this conclusion is being honored. Mr. Baker, like other chiefs of
staff before him, showed no sign of constraining his campaign-related
activity. The reason this purported rule may have so little effect appears
to be threefold. First, as already mentioned, it is often difficult to
disentangle campaign activity from governing activity. Second,
according to a number of members from the White House Counsel's
office, the law in this area is itself "fuzzy" in establishing what kinds of
activity are legal and what are illegal. Indeed, this fuzziness is reflected
in the two positions adopted by the White House Counsels of the Carter
and Bush administrations. The former stated it would be illegal to use
government assets for political purposes; the latter described this only
as an ethical norm. Finally, even assuming there are limits to what can
legally or ethically be done from the White House, enforcement is
virtually nonexistent due to the absence of any White House office
interested in enforcing such a rule.

Nevertheless, fearing the opposition's accusations of abuse of
taxpayers' money, the White House treats these issues seriously. One
example from the Clinton administration illustrates their concern:

> Crowded into the White House basement suite are four phones, two
> fax machines, two cellular phones, two computers and two pagers.
> Half the equipment is government. Half is paid for by President
> Clinton's reelection campaign. Campaign business is to be done on
> the campaign phones, faxes and computers; government business on
> government equipment.[81]

So while there is no enforcement mechanism per se within the White House, presidents and their staff take the issue seriously and go to great lengths to avoid taxpayer subsidization of campaign expenses.

In addition to the White House staff, the First Lady has also played a role in campaigning. This role, however, is a recent phenomenon and varies from administration to administration. For instance, though Mamie Eisenhower campaigned, she typically accompanied her husband. Lady Bird Johnson, however, was more independent and active.[82] In a period of four days, she made forty-seven speeches at sixty-seven stops.[83] Pat Nixon played a role in her husband's reelection effort as well. Though she was privately unenthusiastic about her husband running for a second term, she "had an even larger role in this campaign."[84] She traveled the country delivering speeches and attending receptions. Betty Ford also campaigned independently and was not shy about making known her feminist perspective on various issues, "While she had no illusions about the tradition of a campaign wife's public visibility being limited largely to goodwill and photo opportunities, she continued to infuse it with espousal of her beliefs."[85] During the primaries when the President assumed the Rose Garden strategy, Betty Ford often acted as a surrogate, campaigning for her husband along with various senators and politicians.

Rosalynn Carter was particularly active and her appearances stretched across the entire four-year term. In her memoirs she conveyed, without much pretense of modesty, the breadth of her activity:

According to the [Washington] Star, I visited 18 nations and 27 U.S. cities, held 259 private meetings and 50 public meetings, made 15 major speeches, held 22 press conferences, gave 32 interviews with individual journalists, had 77 hours of briefings, attended 83 official receptions and social functions, held 26 special-interest and group meetings at the White House, spent more than 300 hours working in mental health, received 152,000 letters and 7,939 invitations, signed 150 photographs a week, and made 16 public appearances around Washington, D.C.[86]

Political scientist Betty Glad noted that Rosalynn's activities required more employees to organize her schedule, ". . . the first lady's White House staff . . . expanded to an all-time high of twenty persons. . . . Eleanor Roosevelt had done her work with three aides."[87] During the election year, Rosalynn's travel schedule was even busier, largely because President Carter was tending to the hostage crisis.

Not only was her participation in the promotion of her husband expansive and unique, but her role in campaign planning and strategy was integral. In the 1976 election, Mrs. Carter frequently campaigned on her own because the Carters thought it made "economic" sense— separately they were able to communicate with more voters. Rosalynn Carter set precedent in the 1976 election for being the first wife of a candidate who tried to sell herself and campaign as the nation's next First Lady. "She was unabashedly running for First Lady, unequivocally, unembarassedly viewing it as a full-time job."[88]

Similarly, Nancy Reagan campaigned vigorously in the 1984 election. "By the time 1984 came around, she crisscrossed the country several times integrating meetings on drug abuse at many stops."[89] It was well known that she also supervised the President's campaign schedule as well as his speechwriting and other facets of the reelection campaign. Nancy Reagan was extremely concerned with the well-being of her husband and sought to make sure that his schedule was not too rigorous and that his advisers were doing what was in his best interest. "The first lady's trespasses into the management of the campaign were the expressions of her angst, not some conscious wish to be imperious or incivil with the help."[90] Nevertheless, such gestures were not well received by the campaign staff. Advisers running the campaign were bothered by her intrusive manner and constant supervision. Apparently her excessive concern ultimately led to her independent campaigning in 1984, ". . . it became a conscious part of their [the staff's] strategy for Reagan's reelection to keep her off the campaign plane."[91]

Barbara Bush, a tremendously popular first lady, reverted to the traditional role of first lady, campaigning with minimal input in strategy. Hillary Clinton, perhaps due to her tumultuous entry into the White House, maintained a similar posture by the time of the reelection campaign. Rather than appear as a policymaker and strategist, Hillary

Clinton was portrayed as the nurturing mother traveling the world with her daughter as they addressed women's issues and causes. In addition, the timely release of her book about children provided another nonpolicy portrayal of the first lady, whose image was initially tarnished by her zealous promotion of health care reform and alleged involvement in the Whitewater and "Travel-gate" scandals. Behind the scenes, however, there were numerous reports of her input in campaign strategy sessions.

Another key figure in the president's reelection campaign is the vice president. Though the role of the vice president is largely dependent on the president he serves, scholars agree that since 1945 a vice president's status has risen dramatically.[92] Vice President Nixon played a highly visible role in Eisenhower's reelection effort:

> The itinerary for the first half of Nixon's nationwide speaking tour, billed as the greatest in political history, commenced on September 18, and covered more than 15,000 miles, penetrating 32 states, taking 14 working days, and ending on October 3 in Philadelphia.[93]

Vice presidents since then, Humphrey, Agnew, Dole, Mondale, Bush, Quayle and Gore, also have participated in reelection campaigning. Theodore White describes Humphrey in 1964 as "a force . . . swinging lustily around the country, spreading happiness and savaging Goldwater."[94] According to Nixon campaign aide, Jeb Magruder, "We felt that Vice President Agnew was one of our most effective surrogates. We used him very frequently; he was on the road during the whole period of the campaign."[95] After Dole was nominated at the Republican convention in 1976, he too campaigned extensively as a surrogate. "Though Ford was not to start campaigning until well past Labor Day, Dole was dispatched at once to start cutting Carter down to size."[96] Vice President Mondale not only campaigned extensively in the reelection campaign, but also played an integral role in campaign strategy. Mondale regularly attended strategy meetings in the White House residence along with President and Mrs. Carter, Hamilton Jordan, Pat Caddell, Tim Kraft, Jerry Rafshoon, Richard Moe (Mondale's chief of staff) and other aides. In 1984, Vice President Bush traveled the country on behalf of Ronald Reagan. "George Bush, meanwhile, was campaigning as the loyal Vice President, and there probably never had been one more loyal."[97] Bush also expressed a strong interest in the strategic aspects of the campaign: "It was his running mate and aspiring heir, George Bush, who devoured polls and demographics and demanded constant briefings."[98]

Bush's successor, Vice President Quayle, also proved to be a visible campaign surrogate. Quayle traveled the country regaling listeners with his conservative dogma, in particular his views on "family values." To some Democratic observers, Vice President Quayle was President Bush's "pit bull," repeatedly attacking the Democratic nominee and the Democratically-controlled Congress.

Vice President Gore not only also assumed an aggressive campaigning role, but was a key strategist. By October of 1995, over a year in advance of the election, one reporter was able to write, "Gore has already weighed in on the 1996 campaign, hitting the road in recent months to urge the president's re-election in highly partisan tones."[99] Just as modern vice presidents are playing a greater role in White House affairs throughout their term, they are also assuming a more influential role in the reelection campaign.

The fact that vice presidents are a major campaign resource is not surprising given their fundamental role as loyal advocate of the president. The job consists primarily of traveling the country defending the president's record and galvanizing support for him. Another reason for the active campaigning by the vice president is that, from a strategic perspective, it is better to have the vice president lashing away against the opponent. Such an approach permits the campaign to attack the opposition while simultaneously allowing the incumbent to retain the presidential aura.

The various elements of short-term election planning—strategy formulation, liaison with the campaign and staff campaigning— demonstrate the degree to which the White House is engaged in reelection planning. It is an event that, according to Ford and Reagan reelection campaign strategist Stuart Spencer, "overwhelms the White House."[100]

CONCLUSION

As this chapter demonstrates, the White House is an integral component of the president's reelection campaign. This discussion of long- and short-term planning activities demonstrates the extent to which the White House is involved in the president's campaign. According to a former Bush staff member, "At a certain level, the distinction between the White House office and the campaign disappears."[101] Such a finding is not surprising given the importance of reelection to the president and staff. With an understanding and appreciation for the White House's influential role in reelection planning, the next chapter explores the campaign's short-term impact on White House operations.

NOTES

1. See Sidney Blumenthal, *The Permanent Campaign*, New York: Simon and Schuster, 1982, and Kenneth W. Thompson, *The Virginia Papers on the Presidency*, (Vol. 4), Washington, D.C.: University Press of America, 1979, which documents an oral history session with former Johnson aide, Jack Valenti.

2. Jeb Stuart Magruder, *An American Life*, New York: Atheneum, 1974, p. 158.

3. Patterson, (1988), p. 87.

4. Charles T. Royer (ed.), *Campaign for President: The Managers Look at '92*, Hollis, NH: Hollis Publishing Company, 1994, p. 184. Quote by William Kristol, Chief of Staff, Office of the Vice President.

5. For students of White House staffing, the question of how to calculate White House staff size is a controversial subject. Various scholars have their own preferred method for counting the number of staff members.

See John Hart (1995), for a discussion of White House staff growth. He notes that the amount of growth is dependent upon how one counts White House staff. On p. 116 he provides four different estimates of staff growth.

6. Jonathan Moore (ed.), *Campaign for President: The Managers Look at '84*, Dover, MA: Auburn House Publishing Company, 1986, p. 103.

7. Interview with Margaret Tutwiler, May 24, 1994.

8. See Samuel Kernell and Samuel L. Popkin (eds.), *Chief of Staff*, Berkeley: University of California Press, 1986.

9. Not only is this question interesting from an academic perspective, but it also piques the attention of the media. Just as the president and his team plan ahead for reelection, the media begin to think about the possible outcome of such races. Polling organizations ask speculative questions about the upcoming presidential race more than three-and-a-half years before the election (Nixon). These questions typically focus on whether the President will run. For example, "Do you think Dwight Eisenhower will or will not be a candidate for president again in 1956? Would you like to see George Bush run for President or not? Based on the Gallup Opinion Index, polling for presidential races began on the following dates: Eisenhower, January 1954; Johnson, September 1965; Nixon, April 1969; Ford, January 1975; Carter, March 1978; Reagan, March 1982; Bush, November 1990; and Clinton, January 1993.

10. Harry S. Dent, *The Prodigal South Returns to Power*, New York: John Wiley and Sons, 1978, p. 229.

11. See David, Goldman and Bain, p. 84.

12. Magruder, p. 155.

13. Charles O. Jones, *The Trusteeship Presidency*, Baton Rouge, LA: Louisiana State University Press, 1988, p. 169.

14. Bonafede, November 18, 1978, p. 1852.

15. "Candidate Registration," based on the Commission regulations in Title 11 of the Code of Federal Regulations, pamphlet published by the Federal Election Commission, Washington, D.C.: September 1985.

16. Information obtained from documents at the Federal Election Commission in Washington, D.C.

17. David et al., p. 85.

18. Evans and Novak, p. 466.

19. Telephone interview with Harry McPherson, April 21, 1992.

20. See Theodore White, *The Making of the President 1972*, New York: Atheneum Publishers, 1973, p. 48.

21. Ibid, p. 49.

22. Ernest R. May and Janet Fraser, *Campaign '72 The Managers Speak*, Cambridge, MA: Harvard University Press, 1973, p. 32.

23. Jules Witcover, *Marathon*, New York: The Viking Press, 1977, p. 13.

24. Elizabeth Drew, *Portrait of An Election*, New York: Simon and Schuster, 1981, p. 123.

25. Ibid.

26. Jonathan Moore (ed.), *The Campaign for President: 1980 In Retrospect*, Cambridge, MA: Ballinger Publishing Company, 1981, p. 47.

27. Moore, (1986), pp. 99–100.

28. Ibid, p. 33.

29. Peter Goldman and Tony Fuller, *The Quest for the Presidency 1984*, New York: Bantam Books, 1985, p. 14.

30. See DNC Announcement, The White House, Office of the Press Secretary, Statement by the President, January 12, 1995.

31. See Jack W. Germond and Jules Witcover, *Wake Us When It's Over*, New York: Macmillan Publishing Company, 1985, p. 87.

32. See *The Gallup Poll Monthly*, September, 1991, p. 21.

33. Royer, p. 18.

34. Ann Devroy, "Talking Points," *The Washington Post*, September 5, 1991, p. A19.

35. Ann Devroy, "Republicans: Bush Wounded Politically," *The Washington Post,* November 17, 1991, p. A1.

36. Richard L. Berke, "The President's Brain Trust Brings Politics to the Table," *The New York Times*, July 21, 1996, p. A1.

37. Dan Balz and Ann Devroy, "Gearing Up for '96," *The Washington Post National Weekly Edition*, December 19–25, 1994, p. 11.

38. White, (1973), p. 62.

39. Interview with Rick Hutcheson, November 29, 1992.

40. Moore, (1986), p. 21.

41. Carter Library document, "Memorandum to President Carter from Hamilton Jordan Regarding Thoughts on the Future," no date, but written shortly before the midterm elections, 1978, p. 2.

42. Telephone interview with Stuart Spencer, April 13, 1992.

43. Dick Kirschten, "Reagan Will Be the Issue," *National Journal*, October 29, 1983, p. 2232.

44. Andrew Rosenthal, "Despite Grip on Nomination Bush Still Gropes for Agenda," *The New York Times*, April 30, 1992, p. A1.

45. Alison Mitchell, "Behind the Cloak of Office, Clinton War Room Is in Gear," *The New York Times*, May 7, 1996, p. C20.

46. Nelson W. Polsby and Aaron Wildavsky, *Presidential Elections*, (8th Ed.), New York: Free Press, 1991, p. 46.

47. Mitchell, May 7, 1996.

48. James A. Barnes, "Along the Campaign Trail," *National Journal*, January 13, 1996, p. 77.

49. In 1988, the total matching fund federal subsidy to any candidate could not exceed $11.6 million. Compare to 1992 when the limit was $13.81 million and in 1996 when the limit was $15.45 million. See Herbert Alexander and Monica Bauer, *Financing the 1988 Election*, Boulder: Westview Press, 1991, p. 10. Data from 1992 and 1996 obtained from Federal Election Commission staff member, Dorothy Yeager.

50. Goldman and Fuller, p. 386.

51. Thomas Cronin, *The State of the Presidency*, (2nd Ed.), Boston: Little, Brown and Company, 1980, p. 43.

52. See Dick Kirschten, "Watson's Reward," *National Journal*, June 28, 1980, p. 1066.

53. Elizabeth Wehr, "Public Liaison Chief Dole Reaches to Outside Groups to Sell Reagan's Programs," *Congressional Quarterly Weekly Report*, June 6, 1981, p. 976.

54. Donald Smith, "Ford Strategy Takes Advantage of Incumbency," *Congressional Quarterly*, February 14, 1976, p. 316.

55. Mitchell, May 7, 1996.

56. Memorandum To: Richard Cheney, From: Robert Teeter, Stu Spencer, Re: Analysis of Early Research, Date: November 12, 1975, obtained from the Gerald R. Ford Library, Chanock files, Box 4, "Teeter".

57. Drew, (1981), p. 129.

58. Off-the-record interview with Carter staff member.

59. Andrew Rosenthal, "White House Sees Trips As Way to Revive Bush," *The New York Times*, March 27, 1992, p. A21.

60. Witcover, p. 85.

61. David Loomis, "Ford Travel: Halfway to a Record," *Congressional Quarterly Weekly Report*, November 8, 1975, p. 2420.

62. Memorandum To: Richard Cheney, From: Robert Teeter, Stu Spencer, Re: Analysis of Early Research, Date: November 12, 1975, obtained from the Gerald R. Ford Library, Chanock files, Box 4, "Teeter".

63. Telephone interview with Stuart Spencer, April 13, 1992.

64. See Larry Light, "Iranian Hostage Incident Prompts a Low-key Start of Carter's 1980 Campaign," *Congressional Quarterly Weekly Report*, December 8, 1979, p. 2774.

65. Dom Bonafede, "Who's He Trying to Kid?," *National Journal*, May 10, 1980, p. 781.

66. Andrew Rosenthal, "Bush's Son Rides Into Town to Review the Campaign," (caption), *The New York Times*, April 10, 1992, p. A27.

67. Memorandum for: Rose Mary Woods, From: H.R. Haldeman, Subject: Political Clearance of White House Guests Lists, Eyes Only, December 23, 1971, obtained from the Nixon project; Box 87, Folder– Lawrence Higby, December 1971, White House Special Files, White House Central Files, H.R. Haldeman, Alpha Name Files: A-Z November–December 1971, Clark MacGregor November 1971–Fred Malek December 1971.

68. Interview with Bill Albers, September 20, 1991.

69. Alison Mitchell, "Building a Bulging War Chest: How Clinton Financed His Run," *The New York Times*, December 27, 1996, p. A12.

70. Interview with Margaret Tutwiler, May 24, 1994.

71. Memorandum (untitled, no date) by Cambridge Survey Research (Pat Caddell) regarding general election strategy (1980), p. 46, obtained at the Carter Library.

72. Memorandum to the A.G. [John Mitchell], EYES ONLY, Obtained from the Nixon Project, Box 46, White House Special Files, White House Central Files; Subject Files: Confidential Files 1969–1974, Folder [CF]PL[Political Affairs 9/1/71–4/30/72; [1971–74].

73. Memorandum for the President, From: Tim Kraft, Subject: White House Liaison with Campaign Committee—Crucial Needs, August 14, 1979, obtained from the Carter Library.

74. Quote from Mary Matalin in Mary Matalin and James Carville with Peter Knobler, *All's Fair*, New York: Random House, 1994, p. 162.

75. Ibid, p. 165.

76. Information obtained from personal interviews with Bush White House staff members David Carney and Daniel Casse.

77. Telephone interview with Stuart Spencer, April 13, 1992.

78. See Carter Papers, "Memorandum for Hamilton Jordan, From: Lloyd Cutler, Subject: Constraints on Political Activity," November 19, 1979, p. 2.

79. Ibid.

80. R.W. Apple, "Baker's Racing to Rescue: Harder Now Than in '88," *The International Herald Tribune,* August 15–16, 1992, p. 3.

81. Ann Devroy, "The Perks of Being President," *The Washington Post National Weekly Edition*, April 15–21, 1996, p. 12.

82. See Carl Sferrazza Anthony, *First Ladies*, (Vol.II), New York: William Morrow, 1991, p. 124.

83. Ibid.

84. Ibid, p. 202.

85. Id., p. 265.

86. Rosalynn Carter, *First Lady From Plains*, New York: Ballantine Books, 1985, p. 173.

87. Glad, Betty, *Jimmy Carter: In Search of the Great White House*, New York: W.W. Norton and Company, 1980, p. 453.

88. Anthony, p. 252.

89. James S. Rosebush, *First Lady, Public Wife*, New York: Madison Books, 1987, p. 113.

90. Goldman and Fuller, p. 350.

91. Ibid.

92. Changes in the selection process, presidential succession and disability brought about by the passage of the Twenty-fifth Amendment also have enhanced their position. Further, changes in the 1960s and '70s expanded their resources—office space in the Executive Office Building, staff increases and various perquisites. For an insightful discussion about the evolution of the Office of the Vice President, see Joseph Pika, "The Vice Presidency: New Opportunities, Old Constraints" in Michael Nelson, (1995), p. 496.

93. Thompson and Shattuck, n.6, p. 247.

94. Theodore White, *The Making of the President 1964*, New York: Atheneum, 1965, p. 351.

95. May and Fraser, p. 243.

96. Witcover, p. 540.

97. Germond and Witcover, p. 488.

98. Goldman and Fuller, p. 33.

99. Juliana Gruenwald, "Campaign: Who's In, Out," *Congressional Quarterly*, October 7, 1995, p. 3084.

100. Interview with Stuart Spencer, April 13, 1992.

101. Interview with Daniel Casse, May 23, 1994.

CHAPTER 3

What Changes When the Campaign Begins?
Short-term Effects

As the previous chapter indicates, the White House plays an integral role in the president's campaign. The campaign demands the attention of the president, White House staff and Cabinet members and consequently alters "business as usual." But what changes when the campaign begins? This chapter identifies six short-term effects associated with the presidential campaign. Such findings are based on a systematic analysis of eight presidential campaigns coupled with information obtained in presidential documents and interviews with former White House staff members.

WHAT CHANGES WHEN THE CAMPAIGN BEGINS?

The quest for the presidency is understandably an awesome task and it is no wonder that many in the White House focus their attention on securing a second term for the president. After all, their future employment depends on a successful campaign. If such an event requires as much advanced preparation and constant White House oversight as the previous chapter suggests, it is also the case that the business of government must temporarily share the stage with the business of campaigning. As a result, the campaign precipitates a staff shuffling or restructuring, alters the substance and amount of staff work, politicizes the decisionmaking process to a greater degree, results in a decline in White House policy initiative, modifies presidential activity by increasing the amount of travel, and diverts Cabinet members' attention away from official business.[1]

Staff Reorganization

The first short-term effect of the campaign is a White House staff reorganization.[2] "Here is where the institution changes. People start to leave the White House to work on the campaign, people change jobs and responsibilities and at the same time the campaign starts to recruit. . . . "[3] There are essentially three primary types of staff changes: (1) those that involve staff members leaving the White House to go work for the campaign, (2) those that involve senior staff assuming new White House positions or altering their realm of responsibility, and (3) those that involve high-level, widely publicized resignations and represent a radical staff restructuring within the White House and Cabinet. In addition, the historical overview indicates that presidents in the postreform era (post '68) tended to undergo major staff restructurings compared to their predecessors, largely because these electoral reforms served to decrease the role of the party in presidential politics, leaving the White House team to accomplish and supervise reelection-related activities.

As Chapter Two indicates, these staff changes usually occur in the third or fourth year of a president's first term. Members of the administration from the Cabinet level on down to the lower staff levels in the White House abandon their government posts. Some staff members are recruited while others volunteer to be transferred to the campaign. Members of executive agencies also leave their positions to work on the campaign. Many of these people who work in the government as political appointees eventually return to campaign politics—the avenue that led to their government positions in the first place.[4] Thus business in both the White House and executive branch is disrupted by the departure of many senior aides. Though there may be a number of reasons for such a change (staff burnout, better opportunities in the private sector), one reason for staff changes is that the White

House is taking on a new project which demands intense attention and careful preparation. In an effort to prepare for the most important event of the first term, the president appoints skilled strategists and loyal colleagues from within the administration to staff the newly established campaign organization.

Beginning with Eisenhower, there was no notable staff reshuffling in the pre-election phase of the first Eisenhower administration. For one, Eisenhower's ambivalence about seeking a second term complicated reelection planning in 1956. Further, his health scares in 1955 and 1956 required that the administration work hard to present a cooperative and smoothly functioning staff and Cabinet so as to allay fears that the sickly Eisenhower was unable to govern. A Cabinet shake-up or staff shuffling in the midst of Eisenhower's illness might have created the perception of disarray in the White House, which in turn, surely would have adversely affected his electoral prospects. It is also important to recall that Eisenhower's reelection campaign was run out of the RNC, thereby diminishing the pressure on the White House staff to take on campaign-related tasks. Consequently, there was much less staff restructuring in preparation for the 1956 presidential campaign than for reelection campaigns in the postreform era.

At first glance, Johnson's staff structure prior to the campaign, like Eisenhower's, appears not to fit the pattern described above either. Instead, LBJ's staff underwent a major turnover after the campaign—in the first year of the 1965 term. However, Johnson's decision to forego significant staff shuffling was motivated by the same considerations that drove some presidents (Ford, Carter and Bush) to make major pre-election staff changes and Nixon and Reagan minor ones. Each was driven by campaign management considerations.

Descriptions of Johnson's staff indicate that in the remainder of the Kennedy term, the staff had a dual quality in that the president's staff consisted of Kennedy holdovers as well as LBJ's own loyalists. Johnson, sensitive to the recent tragedy, was careful not to offend the Kennedy team, so he allowed them to remain in the White House and at the DNC. "It was an assemblage of staff support that had two goals: the election of Johnson and the passage of a legislative program that built upon Kennedy's."[5] It was only after these goals were achieved (late

1965–66) that many Kennedy appointees departed and LBJ brought in his own people.

In the aftermath of the 1968 electoral reforms, the Nixon administration launched the first candidate-centered campaign and, as predicted, preparation for this event involved a pre-election campaign staff shuffling. These changes began with Jeb Magruder leaving the White House Office of Communications to establish the national campaign organization and triggered a minor exodus from the White House, "He [Jeb Magruder], political operations chief Harry S. Flemming, fundraiser Hugh Sloan and several other key people . . . came directly from the White House staff."[6] By April of 1972, seventeen of twenty-three senior CREEP members came from the White House staff or administration.[7] In addition, others with varying degrees of involvement in the campaign remained in the White House. "Several other presidential aides—among them Harry S. Dent, Robert H. Finch, Charles W. Colson and Bryce Harlow—were also directly involved in campaign activities while remaining at the White House."[8] Once the campaign was in full swing, Attorney General John Mitchell and Commerce Secretary Maurice H. Stans also joined the reelection campaign. Interestingly, both men assumed the same roles they played in the 1968 election, campaign manager and chief campaign fundraiser, respectively. In a 1972 *Congressional Quarterly* table listing "Republican Campaign Officials," the campaign director, deputy campaign directors (three) and press director were all former White House staff members. Once Mitchell resigned his position as campaign manager, Clark MacGregor, head of White House congressional relations, assumed Mitchell's position. Unlike Presidents Ford and Carter, Nixon refrained from forcing Cabinet resignations until five weeks after the election.[9]

President Ford, like President Johnson, inherited his position but unlike Johnson, Ford experienced a pre-election staff restructuring. In the wake of Watergate and the ensuing pardon of Richard Nixon, President Ford faced an extremely difficult presidential campaign and instigated a Cabinet shakeup prior to the election. In November of 1975, President Ford asked for the resignations of Defense Secretary James R. Schlesinger, CIA Director William E. Colby, and Assistant to the President for National Security Affairs Henry Kissinger. [10] And, like his successor, President Carter, President Ford's shake-up was electorally motivated. Concerned about "public divisions" within the Administration and the perception that he was being overshadowed by Kissinger, Ford sought to demonstrate that he was fully in command. [11] This shake-up extended to the White House staff; Donald Rumsfeld (Ford's chief of staff) assumed the role of Defense Secretary and Richard Cheney inherited the chief of staff position. And at roughly the same time as this Cabinet shake-up, Ford pressed for Vice President Rockefeller's withdrawal from the 1976 ticket. According to Robert Hartmann, a Ford speechwriter, Rockefeller's withdrawal did not accomplish what it was supposed to: ". . . to discourage Reagan's entry into the race and appease his right-wing supporters." [12] The Cabinet shake-up and vice presidential withdrawal (also known as the Halloween Massacre) were part of a general effort by Ford to strengthen his presidential image in time for the election.

In the case of President Carter, one might expect a similarly drastic staff alteration because of his precarious electoral standing:

> While changes among presidential personnel are nothing new or surprising, the movement of Carter staffers began accelerating this year, presumably in response to the President's continuing slide in the public opinion polls, the criticism of Carter's leadership capability and *the realization that the 1980 election was approaching.* [13]

Indeed, in comparison to President Reagan, the Carter administration's staff reorganization was marked by a series of dramatic Cabinet resignations as well as a staff migration from the White House to the campaign. In the summer of 1979, President Carter retreated to Camp David, met with citizens (in and out of government) to hear their grievances and reassessed the direction of his presidency. Subsequently, President Carter asked thirty-four Cabinet members and senior White House staff members to submit letters of resignation. Ultimately, six of the twelve Cabinet positions were turned over to new leadership. [14] Not surprisingly, this move provided the President with significant political opportunities. "In rearranging his Cabinet, the

President managed to satisfy the corporate community, Jews, Catholics, blacks, women, Italians and the big cities."[15]

Furthermore, the Carter shake-up proved to be of symbolic importance, demonstrating his decisiveness and willingness to take strong action in order to reestablish his command of the executive branch. "The Cabinet shuffle was provoked, in large measure, by the traditional rivalry between the Cabinet and the White House and by the desire of Carter and his senior assistants to strengthen their grip on the federal bureaucracy."[16] Others speculated that Carter engineered this shake-up for purely electoral reasons. According to Joseph Califano, Carter told the Cabinet, "'I intend to run for office and I intend to be reelected.' To get ready for this effort over the next eighteen months, personnel changes will be made in the Cabinet and the White House staff."[17] Carter was true to his word; one of the casualties, James R. Schlesinger, Secretary of Energy was thought to have been a "political liability because of long gas lines and an approaching reelection campaign."[18]

In addition to remaking his Cabinet, Carter also revamped the White House staff. At roughly this same time, Hamilton Jordan was formally appointed chief of staff. Initially, Carter refused to appoint a chief of staff when he entered the White House in 1977 because of the negative connotations associated with this post. More specifically, some observers associated Nixon's downfall to his powerful Chief of Staff, H.R. Haldeman. Over the course of the term, however, the Carter White House was plagued by charges of disorganization, so the President sought to minimize such criticism by appointing a single staff member to act as a gatekeeper and supervisor of White House staff. Furthermore, as reelection loomed in the not so distant future, tightening the reins in the White House became an attractive alternative. In the fall of 1980, Chief of Staff Hamilton Jordan moved to the campaign leaving Jack Watson as the acting chief of staff. In addition, other White House staff members including Tim Kraft of the Office of Political Affairs and Personnel and several members of the Congressional Relations staff moved their offices to the campaign headquarters.

The Reagan administration, operating under a different electoral vantage point, did not undergo a drastic staff reorganization as the reelection campaign got underway. Perhaps the most visible departure was Ed Rollins along with other members of the Office of Political Affairs. In Rollins' words, "Once it was determined that I could basically withstand a campaign, the decision was finally made to send me out and just move the entire White House political office out."[19] Though none of the other senior advisers left the White House, many had their duties substantially altered. For instance, Chief of Staff Jim Baker became increasingly involved in strategy formulation. Richard Darman, Assistant to the President and Deputy to the Chief of Staff, also played a major role in the reelection effort; his position became "more political than it had been in the first two years of the administration."[20] And Michael Deaver, the senior aide responsible for Reagan's public image, naturally was more involved in the campaign.

In marked contrast, the Bush staff organizational transformation began with a shuffling of senior aides. In December 1991, roughly two months before the Iowa caucus and the start of the campaign, Chief of Staff John Sununu was replaced by Samuel Skinner, formerly Secretary of Transportation, and with him came an overhaul of the White House staff structure. Chief of Staff Skinner called on business consultant Eugene Croisant to conduct a thorough review of the White House focusing on organizational efficiency. Shortly thereafter, a staff restructuring occurred and was couched in terms of improving domestic policymaking.[21] Skinner's reorganization had another goal in mind, ". . . he is clearly moving toward important changes in personnel and organization designed specifically *to rejuvenate George Bush's sagging re-election prospects*."[22] The state of the economy was a central campaign issue and the White House responded by reorganizing, bringing new people to the White House and setting up a Policy Coordinating Group.[23] The intent of this group was to coordinate domestic, social and economic policy, much as the National Security Council was supposed to have done in foreign affairs.

In addition to changing the staff structure, the new chief of staff brought with him some of his own staff members from the Department of Transportation, shifted White House staff members already in place to new positions and added key Republicans to oversee various activities. Press Secretary Marlin Fitzwater took on the responsibility of overseeing communications efforts. After Skinner conducted a long, drawn-out search for a Communications Director, Fitzwater accepted the position with great reluctance.[24] "Fitzwater's added responsibilities—he will remain as President Bush's chief spokesman—are part of Chief of Staff Samuel K. Skinner's effort to revamp the president's policymaking and communications apparatus as the reelection campaign begins."[25]

In an attempt to formulate a coherent domestic policy before the campaign began, the Bush administration also recruited Clayton Yeutter, then RNC chairman, to "fill gaping holes in its policy and public relations operations for the reelection campaign."[26] According to Mr Yeutter, however, ". . . it was just too late. . . . You just can't change the policy environment and the general public's perception of your policies and the adequacies or inadequacies thereof in that short period of time. So it was too little too late."[27] Another addition, Sherrie Rollins, a private sector consultant, was appointed head of public liaison and intergovernmental relations.[28]

Such staff restructuring, however, apparently did not have its desired effect. By July of 1992, in the wake of a successful Democratic convention and a 20–30 point deficit in early polls, word surfaced that the President would solicit the assistance of his friend, aide and five-time presidential campaign strategist, Secretary of State James Baker.[29] On August 13, President Bush formally announced that James Baker would move to the White House to become chief of staff and senior counselor to the president.

Similar to Skinner's arrival in the White House, several other White House posts changed hands as a result of Mr. Baker's entrance. "Four other pivotal jobs in the White House, including those of deputy chief of staff and the directors of communications, policy planning and political affairs, will go to Mr. Baker's top State Department aides, completing the most extensive personnel shakeup of the Bush presidency."[30] Thus as election day grew near and the President's ratings grew sour, Bush sought to boost the campaign by moving the Secretary of State and his top aides to the White House.

This drastic shift of responsibilities from international affairs to domestic affairs and campaign politics demonstrates the paramount importance that presidents place on their reelection. President Bush, anxious about his faltering reelection campaign, forthrightly removed a central figure in his administration from the hotbed of international politics and placed him in a purely political position.

In the case of Bush, the initial staff restructuring may have been due in part to the arrival of a new chief of staff. However, many of the staff changes were likely to have been designed with a specific eye to renewing President Bush's domestic policy image in time for the November election. By the summer of 1992, it was clear that White House staff changes were made in an effort to salvage a struggling reelection campaign. Such staff changes in the Bush White House during the 1992 campaign made for dramatic headlines, but are not unusual, as the previous section demonstrates.

President Clinton's staff restructuring differed from that of his predecessor, George Bush, in that major changes occurred earlier and were more frequent. Staff restructurings in the Clinton administration occurred in three waves: (1) within the first five months of the administration, (2) after eighteen months, and (3) in response to the disastrous midterm election results and the forthcoming reelection campaign.

The first major set of staff changes occurred less than five months into the Clinton administration under a barrage of criticism for its disorganized, verdant behavior. The repeated and highly visible bungling of major Cabinet appointments resulted in the portrayal of an inept and callow White House staff. In an attempt to salvage his administration early in the game, President Clinton oddly enough called on a Republican, David Gergen, known for his communications savvy. A former aide to Presidents Nixon, Ford and Reagan, Gergen was brought in to beef up the communications office which at the time was deemed to be the source of Clinton's problems. As a result, key campaign operative George Stephanopoulos was removed from his high-visibility post as White House communications director and named a Senior Adviser to the President for Policy and Strategy. In addition, there were a number of internal adjustments. Campaign fundraiser Rahm Emanuel was moved from his position as Director of the Office of Political Affairs to Deputy Communications Director. Campaign adviser Mark Gearan moved from his position as Deputy Chief of Staff to Communications Director. Long-time Arkansas colleague Bruce Lindsey moved from the Director of Personnel to presidential Policy Adviser. And Roy Neel left the Vice President's staff to become the Deputy Chief of Staff.

But even after the arrival of David Gergen and the initial impression that the president's shop was in order, more staff departures occurred during that first year. Howard Paster, Assistant to the President for Congressional Relations departed. Regina Montoya left her position as Assistant to the President for Intergovernmental Affairs. While these staff changes reflect only those at the most senior level, it is important to point out that such senior-level changes produce a "domino effect," in which several members of the same office depart en masse. And despite President Clinton's restructuring, criticism of the White House organization continued.[31]

A mere eighteen months into the Clinton administration, amidst continued criticism, the President took a far bolder move. Chief of Staff Thomas F. McLarty, a longtime Clinton confidant and childhood friend, was replaced by OMB director Leon Panetta. McLarty was retained as a senior adviser with unspecified functions, while Panetta's assistant Alice Rivlin became the new director of the OMB. At the same time, in an effort to overcome criticism of the Clinton foreign policy, Gergen was moved to the State Department to advise Secretary of State Warren Christopher.[32]

Much like the Carter administration, the Clinton administration was criticized for having too many hometown buddies on the staff with too little experience and not enough control from the top. Panetta was brought on board to bring maturity, discipline and Washington experience to the White House staff. Hoping to revive his administration, President Clinton gave Panetta carte blanche to reshape the White House organization and, subsequent to his promotion, various high-level resignations occurred: Mark Gearan, the communications director was replaced by Don Baer; Dee Dee Meyers, the Press Secretary, was replaced by Michael McCurry; and Joan

Baggett, director of Political Affairs, was replaced by Douglas Sosnick. Finally, Panetta sought to rein in the political consultants (Stanley Greenberg, James Carville, Paul Begala and Mandy Grunwald) by requiring them to report first to Harold Ickes, the deputy chief of staff, rather than President Clinton.[33]

The initial feedback on Panetta's performance was positive, "Panetta himself spent a lot of time with the President, and the effects of his influence were soon seen—in a more disciplined Clinton."[34] In the wake of disastrous midterm results, however, President Clinton looked outside the White House for assistance and called upon Republican political consultant, Richard Morris. So rather than shaking up the White House staff yet again, President Clinton moved beyond the confines of the West Wing. Certainly other presidents have consulted outside advisers (Carter-Pat Caddell, Reagan-Stuart Spencer, Bush-Bob Teeter), but the purported amount of input from Mr. Morris on all matters, both governing and campaigning, was thought to be unprecedented:

> Morris has become, in the views of several administration officials
> and outside Democrats, a hidden hand in policy formulation and
> public performance in the Clinton White House and a reminder that
> however much Clinton pledges an orderly policymaking operation, in
> times of trouble, he grabs for new lifesavers wherever they are . . . As
> one source put it, 'It's like a one-man coup.'[35]

In addition, the bipartisan nature of Morris' client portfolio stirred up controversy amongst Washingtonians and some observers detected staff resentment toward President Clinton's new confidant; indignation which manifested itself in the form of public criticism. But while his presence created problems for the administration, oddly enough Morris resigned his position for other reasons. Near the end of the Democratic convention, a tabloid revealed Morris' long-time affair with a prostitute, forcing him to vacate the White House on a rather scandalous note.

President Clinton's staff reorganizations are not in and of themselves uncommon, but the timing and frequency were atypical.

Generally speaking, major staff adjustments occur after the midterm elections and do not involve the inclusion of opposition party members (Gergen and Morris). In the case of Clinton, there were three waves of reorganization—waves which coincided with fierce public criticism or crises (health care debacle, midterm election results). Furthermore, his restructuring may have been less a function of the forthcoming campaign than an attempt to salvage his faltering administration and ultimately his legislative agenda. So rather than realign the staff in anticipation of the campaign, President Clinton could not afford to wait given the political scandals (Whitewater, Travelgate, Vince Foster's suicide) and legislative debacles (health care reform, the crime bill). He was forced to make drastic changes well in advance of the reelection campaign. Nevertheless, he managed to assemble a team of campaign-savvy senior staff members by the time the election season began.

In sum, the preceding historical overview demonstrates the degree and manner in which presidents reorganized their staffs in the months before and during the election campaign. The most substantial staff restructuring occurred in those post-reform administrations in which public support was weakest—the Ford, Carter and Bush campaigns. (Ironically, none of these administrations appeared to operate more effectively after their shake-ups.) Less significant staff changes were made by Nixon and Reagan because their electoral positions were more secure. And while Clinton made significant staff changes, they occurred well before the election. Finally, in the cases of Johnson '64 and Eisenhower, there were no drastic staff alterations, in part because such changes did not serve their electoral needs.

Substance and Amount of Staff Work

The president's reelection campaign also affects the substance and amount of work that staff members must accomplish in the final year of the term. For instance, in an election year, the chief of staff plays two roles: linchpin between the campaign and the White House, and chief political strategist. These additional tasks are formidable and force the chief of staff to alter his priorities, substituting campaign-related work for the business of government. The campaign becomes a preoccupation for the chief of staff, and everyday decisions are made in light of this event and its potential impact on the president's electoral standing.

Additionally, there is a heightened sense of political sensitivity in the White House, particularly for those staff members who deal with constituents and elected officials. White House offices like Public Liaison, Political Affairs and Intergovernmental Affairs become even more attuned to the political climate and turn their energies toward garnering support for the president. According to the director of the Bush Office of Political Affairs, "In the first two years, your major client, if you will, is the party . . . the last two years or whenever you start your campaign up, your major client is the reelection campaign. So it changes [your] role drastically."[36] Holding policy briefings, entertaining key constituents and making decisions which might engender support for the president are common occurrences during an election year. Another Bush official who served as Deputy Director of Cabinet Affairs indicated, "Because of my position at the White House, I had a dual role . . . I spent a lot more time on campaign things."[37] Not surprisingly, the workload in the press and scheduling offices increases substantially once the campaign season begins.[38] According to former Press Secretary Marlin Fitzwater, "The workload multiplies by tenfold. . . . The dynamics of the press office changes in the sense that the press is the messenger of the opposition. It is an adversarial context—the margin of error gets much smaller."[39] The press office must be prepared to respond and react to campaign events in addition to the routine press releases. In addition, the number of scheduling requests multiplies and the scheduling office must interlace the president's business-related schedule with the campaign schedule. According to a Bush White House staff-turned-campaign-staff member, ". . . there is more intensity in the scheduling office during the campaign because it is more difficult to coordinate with the RNC, the campaign and the White House."[40]

An additional example of an increased workload concerns speechwriters and policy advisers who often contribute to the president's campaign stump speeches or more focused policy addresses and position papers. Their work expands beyond the daily dosage of official speeches to include campaign-related addresses as well.

Heightened Politicization

A third short-term effect of campaign planning is the heightened politicization of the decision-making process. According to a former Bush staff member, ". . . starting the second half of '91, everything starts to take on a much more political tone."[41] Another veteran of the Reagan and Bush reelection campaigns indicated, "It is a more politically charged environment."[42] And a Carter senior staff member stated, "During the campaign, things change dramatically because every political story has a reelection dimension and therefore everything you work on has that potential."[43] Manifestations of this heightened politicization come in the form of policy reversals, highly visible foreign policy trips and the strategic doling out of government largesse. Examples abound from administrations both Republican and Democratic.

The primacy of a politicized decisionmaking process is explained by one Republican strategist. "'Once he [Bush] has a campaign team in place, the politics will end up driving the policy. . . . They will tell him that certain governmental actions are necessary if he's going to be reelected.'"[44] This sentiment suggests that without a proper "election alteration" of policy decisions, the president will lose. In March of 1992 a Bush official stated, "The domestic side of the White House and the political operation are really driving things in a way they never did before."[45] One example of heightened politicization was provided by a White House staff member:

> It's certainly true that you become more sensitive during the campaign because every stupid little thing is being used by your opponent, and I think you saw this with the National Endowment for the Arts . . . [Pat] Buchanan was giving Bush a hard time with the NEA and Bush was unable to defend Frohnmeyer [NEA Director] or defend what the NEA had done. He thought he'd be tough and fire

him. And I think that's an example of how an election year forces action.[46]

Another bold example of politics driving policy was President Bush's freeze on the issuance of government regulation, when in the previous three years he signed major pieces of legislation (e.g. the Clean Air Act, the Americans with Disabilities Act) which generated vast new regulation.[47] This practice became even more common as President Bush's rankings in the polls continued to decline just two months before the election. In early September, shortly after the arrival of James Baker as chief of staff, the Bush administration announced a slew of policy reversals: the sale of combat jets to Taiwan and Saudi Arabia, the willingness to modernize the M1 tank and the Osprey V22 aircraft, the rebuilding of hurricane-damaged Homestead Air Force Base in Florida (which in 1991 was almost closed as a result of an independent commission study), additional disaster relief for farmers, and increased subsidies for wheat exports.[48] The Bush administration denied any political motivation. According to one news account, "The White House yesterday defended as 'good government' and 'good politics' the largesse showered on the defense industry and on U.S. farmers by President George Bush during his campaign swing on Wednesday."[49] Others took a more skeptical view claiming that the ploys were an attempt to "buy votes" in disregard of budgetary or foreign policy consequences. These gestures shed light on the intensely political atmosphere which permeates White House decision-making processes during an election year.

President Reagan was accused of altering policy for reelection purposes almost two years before the election:

In the spring of 1983 with President Reagan the least popular of any president by the end of his first two years, many Republican senators who had been Reagan's cheerleaders just a year earlier began carping that *the president was shying away from tough budget cuts in deference to an election nearly two years away.*[50]

And in 1984, a point at which President Reagan had not yet met with any leaders of the Soviet Union, the White House arranged a meeting with Andrei Gromyko in September of 1984. According to Richard Darman, "I think, unquestionably, we viewed it as favorable politically, but again it was not entered into for political reasons."[51] Though members of the White House denied the political overtones, it was rather curious that the Reagan White House waited three and one-half years before arranging to meet with a leader from the Soviet Union. Interestingly, this meeting was arranged subsequent to criticism from the Mondale camp that President Reagan was the only modern President who had not met with a Soviet leader. Emphasizing foreign policy and diplomacy in an election year is a common practice because it is almost always a weakness for the opponent.

Politicized decisionmaking can also come into play when presidents award grants, contracts and other government resources to electorally strategic states or key political allies. During the Nixon administration, a staff member (Fred Malek) was specifically assigned to coordinate this effort.[52] President Carter was notorious for doling out grants to key primary states shortly before the election. Consider the following quotes:

> Thus, when the Small Business Administration decided, just before the Maine precinct caucuses and the New Hampshire primary, to designate five New England states an 'economic dislocation area' because of the lack of snow this winter, enabling businesses to receive low-cost loans . . . it was arranged that New Hampshire's governor, Hugh Gallen, make the announcement, and stories about it were in the papers while Vice-President Mondale and Mrs. Carter were campaigning in the area.[53]

> In the week before the Florida presidential-preference caucuses, for example, the administration announced a number of federally funded projects, including two in Miami, a new Job Corps center and a tourism project in the Cuban community.[54]

To generate support for his reelection campaign, President Carter also made use of a "loophole" in an existing law to provide thousands of government jobs throughout the country:

> Carter also used a loophole in his new Civil Service Reform Law to keep presidential patronage alive in the hiring of 275,000 temporary workers needed to conduct the 1980 census. In March, 1979, in accordance with a provision allowing the President under exceptional circumstances to waive the prohibition against patronage hiring, Carter directed the Census Bureau to hire census employees as much as possible from the neighborhood in which they would work.[55]

Though this action did not require Carter to declare any change in policy positions, it represents the politicization of the grant process which often occurs in the midst of a reelection campaign.

Perhaps the best example of election-motivated decisionmaking during the Clinton administration was the administration's treatment of California.[56] Having narrowly won a state rich in electoral votes in 1992, Clinton was instructed to hang on to it or risk a California defeat in 1996. He took such advice to heart as evidenced by the following actions: the Small Business Administration revised its rules to increase the size of loans that quake-damaged businesses could get and to expand the pool of eligible companies; in terms of economic policies, California was awarded twenty-five to thirty percent—more than any other state—of $1 billion distributed by the technology reinvestment project; the Golden State also benefitted from the administration's efforts to expand foreign trade, making it easier for Silicon Valley companies to sell their products abroad; and finally, in the wake of military base closures, the Clinton administration installed an Air Force maintenance center near the targetted base so that jobs would not disappear.[57]

The doling out of government resources is, in many cases, a well orchestrated effort. For example, in 1984, Jim Baker appointed Richard Darman to oversee efforts to bring government resources to bear for the benefit of the campaign. "Richard Darman . . . served as the conduit for programs and proposals that could be exploited for political gain.

Whenever the campaign team saw the need for action by the administration, it was Darman who knew how to get the government machinery moving."[58] The Bush administration introduced a more sophisticated means of doling out federal "goodies." In 1992, the Bush administration introduced a "funnel" system to take advantage of executive branch resources.[59] This system was a coordinated effort between the White House and various departments to dispense political "goodies" in a strategic manner:

> Each Government agency has a 'campaign contact,' a Federal employee who can supply information to the campaign and arrange political speeches and travel by agency officials. Likewise, the White House has agencies review campaign literature for accuracy and consistency with official Administration positions. Mr. Bush boasts about the fruits of such cooperation, which include Federal money and regulatory actions intended to please voters in politically important states.[60]

This system enabled Bush to make New Hampshire the recipient of a beneficial Small Business Administration program two months prior to the 1992 New Hampshire primary.[61] In the early days of the general election, the Bush team played the patronage card to a large degree:

> Struggling to overcome poll leads held by the Democratic nominee, Governor Bill Clinton of Arkansas, Mr. Bush has used his powers as incumbent to hand out benefits to various voting blocs in recent days.[62]

The Bush strategy introduced a more efficient means of using federal funds for electoral advantage, but the underlying strategy was not new. According to Reagan and Bush White House staff member, Margaret Tutwiler,

> Sure, you play Santa Claus. All presidents do. And those that use it effectively do very well in those states. Why? It affects people's jobs. It can make a difference.[63]

In addition to transforming government resources to election-year patronage, the president can also tinker with the economy in an attempt to gain support. Edward Tufte claims that "an incumbent administration ... may manipulate the short-run course of the national economy in order to improve its party's standing in upcoming elections."[64] Though short-run manipulation may prove beneficial, successful manipulation is not sustainable. According to George C. Edwards, "The prospects of success for these efforts, however, especially in the long run, are not great."[65]

Observers of the presidency are well aware of these politicized activities. According to John Crittenden:

> Incumbents have taken advantage of the presidency to further their reelection cause in important ways. Thus, Harry Truman called a special session of a Congress dominated by the opposition party to dramatize disagreements with it.[66]

Politicized decision making, allocation of government resources for political gain and, to a lesser degree, strategic manipulation of the economy are all activities associated with modern presidential campaigns.[67] These examples merely reflect the paramount importance of reelection and the concomitant willingness to alter policies in hopes of bringing benefit to the reelection campaign.

Declining Policy Initiative

Acknowledging the boundaries of presidential involvement in the reelection campaign itself, it is critical to point out the policy implications of such involvement. Consider the following quotes:

> Within the White House there is less emphasis on issues, fewer decisions coming to the president. The president is distracted by the campaign—lots of travel ... The reality is that the White House pretty much comes to a stop. By the time the Republican convention was over and the [Clinton/Gore] bus trip was over George Bush

decided, 'Maybe we waited too long. Maybe we should've abandoned the process of governing earlier.'[68]

Bush Press Secretary, Marlin Fitzwater

The White House could not get into campaign mode, they could only operate in governing mode, and you don't govern during a campaign year.[69]

Mary Matalin, Bush/Quayle Political Director

While there is little doubt that the campaign interrupts business as usual in the White House, its actual effects on governance are not entirely clear.[70] These quotes by Marlin Fitzwater and Mary Matalin might come as a shock to many observers of the presidency. While many suspect that the White House is preoccupied by the campaign, few would expect business to come to a halt. Research indicates, however, that despite presidents' best efforts to juggle both election and governing activities, the reelection campaign takes its toll on the business of policymaking. According to a Bush staff member,

It is very hard to govern and campaign at the same time. Everything changes. Nobody cares about anything except reelection. It is hard to focus on domestic issues. There are no new legislative programs. The initiative dries up after January [of the election year]. Policy analysts fall by the wayside. The White House focuses on those things they **have to** deal with—foreign policy and getting reelected . . . Virtually nothing gets done.[71]

And a Reagan staff member indicated:

Policy in terms of making policy tends to atrophy towards the end of an administration. You can't create new policy in a short period of time especially when everything has more of a political appearance.[72]

Legislative Proposals Transmitted to Congress by the President[73]

President	1st Year of Term	2nd Year of Term	3rd Year of Term	4th Year of Term	Difference 4th–3rd
Johnson	**	**	*0	6	n/a
Nixon	17	12	8	3	−5
Ford	**	**	*10	6	−4
Carter	21	8	8	4	−4
Reagan	2	10	25	8	−17
Bush	10	6	6	22	16
Clinton	9	4	8	3	−5

** Did not serve.

* Partial term.

Not surprisingly, if policy innovation "dries up" so too do presidential legislative initiatives. A look at the number of White House legislative initiatives transmitted to Congress indicates a net decline from the first year to the fourth year (with the exception of President Bush). Note that the data for President Reagan may be misleading because the records indicate only two presidential requests during the first year of Reagan's term. In fact, the single Economic Recovery Tax Act contained several pieces of legislation presented as a single "package" of legislation. Apparently the Office of Legislative Reference treated this as a single legislative request resulting in the appearance of a relatively inactive first year in office. Perhaps a more revealing and accurate reflection of the decline in legislative activity during the fourth year of Reagan's term is the fact that Reagan's eight proposals in 1984 are seventeen less than the previous year (1983), and two less than the proposals introduced in 1982.

Another anomaly within this list is the vast increase in legislation initiated during the last year of President Bush's term. This increase could, in part, be due to White House strategists' realization that President Bush was frequently characterized as the "Foreign Policy President" at a time when Americans were increasingly concerned with domestic policy, particularly the economy. Recall that in December of

1991, President Bush called on Clayton Yeutter, then RNC chair, to move to the White House to head the domestic policy team. This staff restructuring and shift in emphasis likely influenced the plethora of legislation emerging from the White House in 1992.

Another indicator of White House policy initiative is the presidential executive order.[74] As President Clinton stated, ". . . one of the things that I have learned in the last two years is that the President can do an awful lot of things by executive action, so that the sum total of the Presidency's impact on the American people at home is not just what happens in the Congress, it also involves what can be done by way of executive action. . . . "[75] Not surprisingly given the trend in White House legislative initiatives, since Eisenhower the number of executive orders has declined from the third to the fourth year in every administration except Clinton, and in some cases (Eisenhower and Reagan) there are dramatic differences between the first and the fourth year.

Decline of Executive Orders During the President's First Term

President	1st Year of Term	2nd Year of Term	3rd Year of Term	4th Year of Term	Difference 4th–3rd
Eisenhower	90	73	65	44	−21
Johnson	**	**	*7	56	n/a
Nixon	61	72	63	55	− 8
Ford	—	29*	67	56	−11
Carter	83	78	77	73	− 4
Reagan	76	63	57	41	−16
Bush	36	43	46	40	− 6
Clinton	57	54	39	47	+8

**Did not serve.
*Partial year.
Source: Lyn Ragsdale, *Vital Statistics on the Presidency*, Washington, D.C.: Congressional Quarterly Press, 1996, pp.342-343. Data for President Clinton obtained from Congressional Research Service via Senator Bob Graham's office.

Generally speaking, the final year of a president's first term is typically a period when few if any new policy initiatives emerge.[76] President Ford's Chief of Staff, Dick Cheney, noted this problem, "If you are in the middle of a tough, knock-down, drag-out campaign, it limits your ability to get things done . . . the issue [SALT Treaty] sort of went on the back burner, so it didn't get mixed up in the campaign, but it [the campaign] did delay and defer policy."[77] Furthermore, a sitting president is reluctant to engage in policymaking, fearing adverse reactions and a subsequent drop in poll ratings.

Change in Presidential and Cabinet Activity

A fifth short-term campaign effect is a change in presidential and Cabinet activity. The chief executive continues to discharge his presidential duties while tending to the multiple demands of the campaign. When asked a question about the ability to handle governmental and campaign-related duties, former President Gerald Ford responded, "I've always believed if you work at it, if you spend sixteen hours a day on the job, you can handle both the politics and the substantive issues that are on the desk in the Oval Office."[78] Spending sixteen hours a day on the job may even be an understatement, particularly in the last phase of the campaign when the president is preparing for presidential debates, participating in last minute, critical, campaign events and crisscrossing the country in the final hours before voters cast their ballots.

One reflection of the change in activity is the amount of presidential travel. This should come as no surprise since newspaper readers are bombarded with campaign stories in which the media follow the candidates across the country on a seemingly endless series of campaign visits. Not only do presidents travel more during the election year, but the destinations are strategically located. A *Christian Science Monitor* article written in December of 1979 reports, "Since July (1979), Mr. Carter has visited 24 of the 50 states—all but six of which happen to be the sites of presidential primaries early next year."[79]

Aside from anecdotal evidence and casual observation, a systematic review of presidential travel obtained from the *Public Papers of the Presidency*, reveals that the number of presidential trips (those which require the president to leave Washington, D.C.) significantly increases in the fourth year of the term.

The exceptions to increased travel are President Eisenhower who suffered health problems during 1956 and President Nixon who adopted the Rose Garden strategy. According to William Lammers:

> Thus for Nixon, as for Eisenhower, the use of the presidency for reelection purposes involved a strategy of avoiding direct campaigning and emphasizing the importance of presidential action.[80]

Presidential Political Travel 1952-1992[81]

President	1st Year	2nd Year	3rd Year	4th Year
Eisenhower	21	29	24	25
Johnson	**	**	*4	144
Nixon	42	61	50	49
Ford	**	*53	102	211
Carter	33	78	65	131
Bush	95	121	92	267

**Did not serve.
*Partial year.
Source: *Public Papers of the Presidency*, Washington, D.C.: Government Printing Office, tabulation from successive volumes.
Comprehensive data for the Clinton administration was unavailable at time of publication.

Corroborating the finding that travel increases in a reelection year, Paul Brace and Barbara Hinckley compare foreign and domestic travel revealing that:

... foreign trips increase as election nears, most of them occurring in the spring of the reelection year, while domestic trips reach their peak in the fall of the election year.[82]

In sum, unless a president makes a deliberate strategic decision not to travel, the typical pattern for presidential travel is that it increases during an election year.[83]

Cabinet Campaigning

It is not just the president who is distracted by the demands of the campaign. Many of the Cabinet members are also asked to tend to campaign-related duties like making appearances across the country on behalf of the president. In two off-the-record interviews, I learned that Jack Kemp, Secretary of Housing and Urban Development during the Bush administration, spent up to one-third of his time (as of April of 1992) campaigning for President Bush. One White House staff member speculated that by the time of the general election, the portion of Kemp's time devoted to campaigning would increase to two-thirds. This same staff member added that, "When the general election season hits, Cabinet business will be replaced with campaign business." The department schedule is by and large cleared to accommodate the needs of the campaign.

Prior to an election, Cabinet members may also be called upon to campaign for the president, to publicize various administrative positions or to allocate discretionary grants to strategically-located constituencies. According to the Special Assistant to the President for Cabinet Affairs in the Bush administration, Daniel Casse, "My job was concerned with what the President and members of the Cabinet spend their time doing and in an election you spend time promoting the President's record and getting the president reelected. That started getting very intense in June of 1992."[84] Select Cabinet members act as presidential surrogates and allow the president to retain the presidential aura while they act as candidate spokespersons, attacking the opposition or vigorously promoting and defending the administration.

In 1980, Labor Secretary Ray Marshall was criticized for neglecting his job. According to the *National Journal*, he replied, "'I've been campaigning since 1977 and I don't intend to stop now."[85] This added responsibility distracts those Cabinet members involved in the campaign from the normal course of business at the department or agency. Demonstrating this departure from the normal business of governing, journalist Elizabeth Drew noted that in 1980, "Cabinet meetings, which once were held weekly, are now infrequent."[86] Certain members of the Cabinet are called on to give numerous speeches and attend various receptions in locations that are strategically beneficial. Members of the Cabinet who tend to national security issues like the Secretary of Defense, the National Security Adviser, Director of the CIA and the Secretary of the State, however, do not participate in campaigning activities. Since the Watergate debacle, the Attorney General has also remained on the periphery of campaign politics. Among those Cabinet members eligible for campaigning, the administration discourages them from travel abroad or speeches before small audiences; in other words, they want to maximize the campaigning potential of the Cabinet by stressing domestic travel and large audiences.

The Cabinet is also known to contribute to the president's reelection campaign by providing useful information that can be used in election speeches. For example, if the president is making a speech on education, policy specialists at the Department of Education can offer substantive input. President Johnson not only called on his Cabinet to campaign, but brought one member to the White House as a speechwriter.[87] "Five weeks before the [1964] election, Wirtz moved quietly from the Labor Department to the Executive Office Building and opened a speechwriting sweatshop that sometimes ran until 2 in the morning."[88] In February of 1976, *Congressional Quarterly* reported that, "Later in the year, a brigade of Cabinet and sub-Cabinet officials, along with sympathetic governors, senators and representatives, will fan out all over the country to campaign for Ford in the Ford committee's 'Advocate Program.'"[89] At one point in February of 1976, President Ford transferred Secretary of Commerce Rogers C.B. Morton to the White House as a domestic/economic adviser and as a liaison to the campaign. When the FEC caught wind of this innovative transfer at taxpayers' expense, Morton left his position and became campaign manager in late March.[90]

This resource, however, is not always utilized, ". . . the Bush team still does not comb the Cabinet agencies for material the President can use in his speeches, a common practice in President Gerald R. Ford's 1976 campaign and President Ronald Reagan's 1984 campaign."[91] Not surprisingly, given its conspicuous emulation and adherence to the Reagan '84 playbook, the Clinton administration utilized its vast resources, "Cabinet departments and agencies have worked with the White House to churn out policy proposals, issues statements and presidential orders—a blizzard of rhetoric, and some occasional substance, designed to help Clinton's message reach voters."[92]

In the Carter administration, Cabinet members' advice and participation was actively solicited. According to Cabinet member Joseph Califano,

> The President sent his staff out, announced that he was going to run, but that nothing would be made public until late this year [1979]. Fritz [Mondale] will meet privately with members of the Cabinet to go over campaign plans, including fundraising and speeches. Jordan and Tim Kraft will be there, and the meeting will work off Jordan's plan and agenda, but he wants each Cabinet member to bring his own agenda and suggestions.[93]

This said in February of 1979, Tim Kraft proceeded to state in the aforementioned meeting:

> . . . each Cabinet officer would be asked to speak at least once a month for the White House, and that each should give a travel schedule to the White House so that political events could be worked in around departmental business. When a Cabinet officer was in a particular city on departmental business, he or she would stay a couple of hours and do an event to help raise money for the Carter campaign.[94]

And at a more specific level, in a memo to President Carter, Hamilton Jordan indicated:

> We need three things from our Cabinet officers and from agency heads: (1) targeted calls to Iowans furnished by our Iowa campaign, (2) Cabinet members to mobilize their talented political appointees and (3) Cabinet members and others to be creative in their efforts to influence the Iowa caucus.[95]

Not surprisingly, some Cabinet members resisted such pressure which resulted in stringent lectures by President Carter. In a memo to the President about a forthcoming meeting with the Cabinet, Hamilton Jordan wrote:

> The tone of the meeting should be straightforward and tough. The Cabinet generally regards the campaign as "somebody else's business," and you should let them know that we are in for the fight of our lives and without everyone helping, we will be in for a very bad time. You might brag a little on Bergland and Marshall who have really done yeoman's service over the past several months. They deserve some special praise.[96]

It makes perfect sense that presidents would ask their Cabinet members to campaign on their behalf. "Despite Republican cries of foul, the [Carter] White House clearly feels that the Cabinet officers are doing exactly what they should be doing."[97] Many of the Cabinet members have close ties to key constituencies and their influence may be of great benefit to the president's reelection campaign. And, from an efficiency perspective, the reelection campaign can reach many more voters when Cabinet members campaign on behalf of the president.[98] Cabinet participation is especially useful when the president adopts the Rose Garden strategy because they can act as campaign surrogates and reach out to designated constituency groups.

A result of this campaign involvement is a decline in policy innovation at the Cabinet level. In July of 1992 when the White House canceled its plan to issue a report on health risks from toxic materials, one news report cited the campaign demands on members of the Cabinet as the reason for cancellation.

'I was skeptical that we could pull it all together before the convention, and that's what happened,' said a senior adviser to the President who insisted on anonymity. 'Cabinet people are out of town all the time now campaigning and it became logistically impossible.'[99]

In a White House memorandum, a member of the Nixon Domestic Council noted,

... Now that the California primary has passed we [the domestic policy staff] propose to devote more of our resources to analyzing the substantive issue positions of the leading Democratic candidates.[100]

The alteration of a department's agenda is not unusual since it is often more beneficial politically to pursue certain policies, particularly if they are ones that will generate favorable publicity:

In December 1979 Secretary of Agriculture Robert Bergland hosted hearings on the issue of preserving the family farm in nine states, six of which were scheduled for presidential primaries early in 1980.[101]

Cabinet members are also advised to steer away from controversial initiatives during an election year and focus on policies designed to appeal to key constituencies. In addition, Cabinet members become increasingly involved in the strategic allocation of grants and other department awards to key primary states. This is not to say that agency business is completely neglected, only that the forthcoming election precipitates a shift in priorities and thus the substance of the Cabinet secretary's business. According to Bush Press Secretary, Marlin Fitzwater, "The Cabinet doesn't have a very aggressive role, but there are changes in terms of substance. Agencies slow down to the point where they've got time on their hands."[102] In short, the election year finds policy analysts becoming opposition researchers and the formulation of new policies retreating to the backburner. Senior aides are immersed in polling data and strategy meetings, while policy analysts are relegated to the task of proofreading campaign policy statements. The sheer maintenance of government becomes the primary goal.

CONCLUSION

It is not surprising that the White House staff, president and Cabinet alter their workload in light of the reelection campaign. While outside campaign strategist Stuart Spencer indicated that the campaign overwhelms the White House, staff insider Marlin Fitzwater responded, "There is no question that the campaign overwhelms the White House."[103] President Carter's political director, Tim Kraft indicated that, "There were twenty-two months where reelection wasn't a preoccupation."[104] Other former White House staff members have described the reelection campaign as "permeating everything" or "preoccupying everybody."

The presidential campaign has a significant short-term impact on the White House staff, the president and the Cabinet. The campaign elicits a structural change within the White House staff organization, increases the staff workload substantially and places a priority on reelection-related work, politicizes decisionmaking to a greater degree, results in a decline in policy initiative, alters the president's activity and diverts Cabinet members' attention from departmental or agency business. As election day approaches, the White House staff, president and Cabinet must learn to adjust and cope with the competing responsibilities of governing and campaigning.

NOTES

1. While some scholars might find it preferable to provide a systematic explanation of how the campaign affects each facet of the presidency or each presidential role (Chief of State, Commander in Chief, Chief Legislator), this

would be extremely difficult to do. One reason is that it is difficult to define "normal" White House operations so that one can then distinguish between "normal" and "campaign-related." So much of what the White House does is reacting to international and domestic events and politics that there is no such thing as "normal" operations. Given this methodological barrier, I have adopted an inductive method of research in which I identify short-term effects within the White House which occur as a result of the presidential campaign.

2. For a detailed overview of reelection-induced staff restructuring, see Kathryn Dunn Tenpas and Matthew J. Dickinson, "Governing, Campaigning and Organizing the Presidency: An Electoral Connection?," *Political Science Quarterly*, volume 112, number 1, Spring 1997, pp. 51–66.

3. Interview with Daniel Casse, May 23, 1994.

4. For more information see Priest, June 18, 1992, p. A21.

5. Redford and McCulley, p. 31.

6. "Nixon Campaign: Mounting A Drive for Another Term," *Congressional Quarterly Weekly Report*, November 27, 1971, p. 2452.

7. U.S. House of Representatives Committee on the Judiciary, White House Staff and President Nixon's Campaign Organizations, (June 1974), p. 5.

8. Ibid.

9. For details, see *Congressional Quarterly Weekly Report*, December 30, 1972, p. 3212.

10. Henry Kissinger held two positions at the same time: National Security Adviser and Secretary of State. He remained in the Ford administration as Secretary of State.

11. Gerald R. Ford, *A Time To Heal*, New York: Harper and Row, 1979, p. 320.

12. Robert Hartmann, *Palace Politics*, New York: McGraw-Hill, 1980, p. 370.

13. Dom Bonafede, "At the White House, You Can't Tell the Players without a Scorecard," *National Journal*, October 6, 1979, p. 1641 (emphasis added).

14. Five cabinet members resigned: Treasury Secretary W. Michael Blumenthal; Energy Secretary James R. Schlesinger; Health, Education and Welfare Secretary Joseph A. Califano, Jr.; Transportation Secretary Brock Adams; and Attorney General Griffin B. Bell. In addition, Patricia Roberts Harris switched from Housing and Urban Development to Secretary of Health, Education and Welfare. See Dom Bonafede, "Carter Turns on the Drama—But Can He Lead?," *National Journal*, July 28, 1979, p. 1237.

15. Dom Bonafede, "The Fallout from Camp David—Only Minor White House Changes," *National Journal*, November 10, 1979, p. 1897.

16. Bonafede, July 28, 1979, p. 1237.

17. Joseph Califano, *Governing America*, New York: Simon and Schuster, 1981, p. 430.

18. Richard E. Cohen, "What to Expect From Carter's New Cabinet," *National Journal*, July 28, 1979, p. 1241.

19. Moore, (1986), p. 100.

20. Ibid., p. 103.

21. See Ann Devroy, "Skinner Reorganizes Personnel," *The Washington Post*, February 28, 1992, p. A1.

22. Kenneth T. Walsh, "Return of Baker and the Handlers," *U.S. News & World Report*, January 13, 1992, p. 31 (emphasis added).

23. See James Gerstenzang, "Early Praise for Skinner Tempered by Complaints," *Los Angeles Times*, April 12, 1992, p. A1.

24. Interview with Marlin Fitzwater, May 19, 1994.

25. John E. Yang, "Fitzwater Appointed PR Coordinator," *The Washington Post*, January 27, 1992, p. A15.

26. Ann Devroy, "Yeutter Offered Top Bush Policy Post As White House Retools for Campaign," *The Washington Post*, January 25, 1992, p. A10.

27. Interview with Clayton Yeutter, May 25, 1994.

28. Ms. Rollins ultimately resigned in June of 1992 when her husband, Ed Rollins, signed on as campaign manager to undeclared, independent candidate, Ross Perot.

29. Ann Devroy, "Baker Said Likely To Resign Post," *The Washington Post*, July 22, 1992, p. A1. See also, Michael Wines, "Baker to Assume White House Post to Run Campaign," *The New York Times*, July 22, 1992, p. A1.

30. Paul F. Horvitz, "Bush Appoints Baker As His Chief of Staff, New Agenda Pledged," *International Herald Tribune*, August 14, 1992, p. 1.

31. For details regarding the first staff shuffle, see Ruth Marcus, "GOP Insider to Be Clinton Counselor," *The Washington Post*, May 30, 1993, p. A1; John M. Broder, "Gergen Reveals He Has Sweeping Power," *Los Angeles Times*, June 8, 1993, p. A16; Michael Kranish, "Clinton to Reduce White House Staff," *The Boston Globe*, February 10, 1993, p. 3; and Carl P. Leubsdorf, "It Can Be Too Much Fun," *The Dallas Morning News*, December 23, 1993, p. 17A.

32. On the 1994 staff shakeup, see Douglas Jehl, "Clinton Shuffles His Aides, Selecting Budget Director as White House Staff Chief," *The New York*

Times, June 28, 1994, p. A1; Michael Kranish, "McLarty out, Panetta in as Clinton Shakes Staff," *The Boston Globe* June 28, 1994, p. 1; Marshall Ingwerson, "Deficit Hawks Rise to the Top in White House," *The Christian Science Monitor,* June 29, 1994, p. 1; and Suzanne Garment, "Starting Over: Is Lack of Focus the Problem,?" *Los Angeles Times,* July 3, 1994, p. M1.

33. See Elizabeth Drew, *On the Edge,* New York: Simon and Schuster, 1994, pp. 420-425.

34. Ibid, p. 423.

35. Ann Devroy, "Republican Adviser Stages a Quiet White House 'Coup'," *The Washington Post,* June 18, 1995, p. A1.

36. Interview with Ron Kaufman, May 25, 1994.

37. Interview with Daniel Casse, May 23, 1994.

38. See John Kessel for a discussion of increasing workload for White House staff, particularly during the Carter administration. *Presidential Parties,* Homewood, IL: The Dorsey Press, 1984, p. 64.

39. Interview with Marlin Fitzwater, May 19, 1994.

40. Interview with David Carney, May 20, 1994.

41. Interview with Daniel Casse, May 23, 1994.

42. Interview with Andrew Card, December 15, 1994.

43. Off-the-record interview.

44. Robin Toner, "Bush Takes Hits From All Sides, Including His Side," *The New York Times,* December 1, 1991, Section IV, p. 1.

45. Rosenthal, March 27, 1992, p. A21.

46. Interview with Daniel Casse, May 23, 1994.

47. See David E. Rosenbaum and Keith Schneider, "Bush is Extending Regulation Freeze with a Fanfare," *The New York Times,* April 29, 1992, p. A22.

48. See "Bush Backs Sale of 150 F-16s To Taiwanese," Compiled by Staff from Dispatches, *International Herald Tribune,* September 3, 1992, p. 1; John Lancaster, "From National Security, An Advantage for Bush, *International Herald Tribune,* September 4, 1992, p. 1; Jurek Martin, "White House Defends Bush Largesse," *Financial Times,* September 4, 1992, p. 18; and Kevin Brown, "Australia Angry at U.S. Subsidized Wheat Plans," *Financial Times,* September 4, 1992, p. 4.

49. Martin, September 4, 1992, p. 18.

50. Samuel Kernell, *Going Public,* Washington, D.C.: Congressional Quarterly Press, 1986, p. 187 (emphasis added).

51. Moore, (1986), p. 190.

52. See Robert Pear, "White House 'Funnel' Gets Help for States with Primaries Nearing," *The New York Times*, March 10, 1992, p. A21.

53. Elizabeth Drew, "A Reporter at Large," *The New Yorker*, April 14, 1980, p. 126.

54. Herbert Alexander, *Financing the 1980 Election*, Lexington, MA: D.C. Heath and Company, 1983, p. 219.

55. Glad, p. 455.

56. For additional examples of the Clinton administration doling out federal largesse, see Michael K. Frisby, "Despite Funding Cuts, White House Finds Ways To Exercise the Power of the Purse To Get Votes," *Wall Street Journal*, October 10, 1996, p. A20.

57. Burt Solomon, "Clinton: California on His Mind," *National Journal*, January 20, 1996, p. 134.

58. Bob Schieffer and Gary Paul Gates, *The Acting President*, New York: E.P. Dutton, 1989, p. 183.

59. The "funnel system" also refers to the Bush administration's failed attempt to limit the number of White House contacts for the campaign as discussed in Chapter Two. Concerned about ethical issues related to staff participation in the campaign, legal counsel C. Boyden Gray initially set a limit on the number of White House staff members who were legally permitted to communicate with campaign staff. According to a campaign staff member, this system broke down shortly after its adoption and thereafter many more staff members were permitted to speak with campaign workers.

60. Pear, March 10, 1992, p. A21.

61. See Maralee Schwartz, Ann Devroy and Helen Dewar, "New Hampshire Aid Challenged," *The Washington Post*, December 18, 1991, p. A18.

62. "Bush Backs Sale of 72 Jet Fighters to Saudis," Compiled by Staff from Dispatches, *International Herald Tribune*, September 12–13, 1992, p. 1.

63. Interview with Margaret Tutwiler, May 24, 1994.

64. Edward R. Tufte, *Political Control of the Economy*, Princeton: Princeton University Press, 1978, pp. 3–4.

65. George C. Edwards, III, *The Public Presidency*, New York: St. Martin's Press, 1983, p. 51.

66. John A. Crittenden, *Parties and Elections in the United States*, Englewood Cliffs, NJ: Prentice-Hall, 1982, p. 239.

67. Interestingly, while news reports have focused on these activities, generally speaking, they have not received much scholarly attention.

68. Interview with Marlin Fitzwater, May 19, 1994.

69. Matalin and Carville, p. 299.

70. Note that presidents are not alone in terms of declining productivity. Members of Congress are less likely to pursue major legislation during an election year; not to mention the fact that Congress is actually in session for less time during a presidential election year. See John Kessel, pp. 63–64.

71. Interview with Marlin Fitzwater, May 19, 1994 (emphasis added).

72. Off-the-record interview.

73. The numbers from Johnson through Carter were obtained from Paul Light's book, *The President's Agenda*, Baltimore: The Johns Hopkins University Press, 1991, p. 42. For subsequent administrations, I obtained data from the same source that Light utilized. Data from the Reagan administration were obtained from the Office of Management and Budget (OMB), Legislative Reference Division Clearance Record, "Status of Administration-Sponsored Legislation Final Report," reviewed on site, December 1991. Data from the Bush administration were obtained via fax from Diane Wells at the OMB Office of Legislative Reference, January, 1995. Data from the Clinton administration were obtained via fax from Jim Murr, OMB Legislative Reference Division, October, 1996.

74. Ruth P. Morgan examines the policymaking effectiveness of the executive order in her book, *The President and Civil Rights*, New York: St. Martin's Press, 1970.

75. Alison Mitchell, "Despite His Reversals, Clinton Stays Centered," *The New York Times*, July 28, 1996, p. A11.

76. A helpful means for accounting for the variation can be found in John Kessel's book, *Presidential Parties*. He identifies four stages which every first-term president experiences (Transition, Midterm Election, Maturing Administration and Reelection). In the process, he explains how the reelection stage affects policymaking (see pp. 63-71). Steven A. Shull, in his book, *Domestic Policy Formation*, reveals similar findings indicating that "Presidents are least assertive and expansive during reelection years." Westport, CT: Greenwood Press, 1983, p. 144.

77. Kernell and Popkin, pp. 101–102.

78. Transcript, "Inside Washington" Interview with President Gerald R. Ford, August 10, 1992, conducted by Richard V. Allen. Transcript obtained from Mark Allen.

79. Peter C. Stuart, "Carter Wields 'Perks' of Office," *Christian Science Monitor*, December 10, 1979, p. 9.

80. William Lammers, "Presidential Attention-Focusing Activities," in *The President and the American Public*, Doris A. Graber (ed.), Philadelphia: Institute for the Study of Human Issues, 1982, p. 162.

81. Presidential "political" travel is defined as travel outside of Washington D.C. in which the president makes formal remarks (which then become part of the *Public Papers of the Presidency*). One exception to this definition is travel to presidential vacation locations like Kennebunkport, Camp David, Plains, San Clemente and Vail which I have omitted from the totals. I have borrowed (and modified) this research approach from William Lammers.

82. Paul Brace and Barbara Hinckley, *Follow the Leader*, NY: Basic Books, 1992, p. 54.

83. Another means of demonstrating increased campaign-related activity is to examine presidential political appearances (or "partisan" appearances). Gary King and Lyn Ragsdale boldly demonstrate the increase in presidential political appearances from Eisenhower through Reagan. See *The Elusive Executive*, Washington, D.C.: Congressional Quarterly Press, 1988, p. 274.

84. Interview with Daniel Casse, May 23, 1994.

85. Dick Kirschten, "Cabinet Government Really Does Work—On the Presidential Campaign Trail," *National Journal*, October 25, 1980, p. 1801.

86. Drew, (1981), p. 131.

87. This action was supposed to be kept under strict secrecy because Johnson feared the public reaction if they were to find out that the Labor secretary was writing speeches instead of tending to the business of the Labor Department. See Evans and Novak, p. 466.

88. Charles Roberts, *LBJ's Inner Circle*, New York: Delacorte Press, 1965, p. 146.

89. Smith, February 14, 1976, p. 315.

90. See Herbert Alexander, *Financing the 1976 Election*, Washington, D.C.: Congressional Quarterly Press, 1979, p. 303.

91. Rosenthal, April 10, 1992, p. A27.

92. John F. Harris, "On the Stump in the Oval Office," *The Washington Post National Weekly Edition*, July 22–28, 1996, p. 12.

93. Califano, p. 419.

94. Ibid at 420.

95. Memorandum, *Eyes Only* To: President Carter, From: Hamilton Jordan, RE: Iowa, dated 1/12/80, obtained from the Carter Library.

96. Memo from the Carter Library, *Eyes Only*, To: President Carter, From: Hamilton Jordan, Re: Cabinet Meeting Tonight, dated November 5, 1979.

97. Kirschten, October 25, 1980, p. 1800.

98. Lyn Nofziger noted in an interview that during an election year, members of the Cabinet may begin to feel somewhat neglected. The focus of government activity is increasingly on the White House and Cabinet members have to pay more attention to White House policy and less to their own agenda. May 5, 1992.

99. Keith Schneider, "White House Drops Plan on Setting Health Risks," *The New York Times*, July 28, 1992, p. A9.

100. Memorandum for John Ehrlichman, Via Ken Cole, From: Ed Harper, Subject: Contender Research, June 9, 1972; Obtained from the Nixon Project, Box 48, White House Special Files, White House Central Files, Subject Files: Confidential Files, 1967–74 [CF] PL/Humphrey [1969–70] to [CF]PL 5-4 Republican Party [1971–74].

101. Alexander, (1983), p. 218.

102. Interview with Marlin Fitzwater, May 19, 1994.

103. Interview with Marlin Fitzwater, May 19, 1994.

104. Interview with Tim Kraft, September 11, 1991.

CHAPTER 4

The President's Campaign Committee

The campaign organization is an additional component of the president's campaign and, unlike the White House and the national party organization, the campaign committee has but one function—to win the presidential election. The independent campaign organization has emerged as a means for presidents to control and supervise the many activities of the presidential campaign which cannot be legally performed in the confines of the White House. Since President Nixon, successive presidents and White House staff members have come to recognize the importance of having a campaign organization which is solely responsible to the president.[1] Rather than delegating such responsibility to the party, which has numerous other responsibilities, presidents seeking reelection prefer to work with an entity over which they have complete control and whose exclusive objective is the reelection of the president.

As previously mentioned, all presidents since Nixon have established their own campaign organization: CREEP, the President Ford Committee, the Carter/Mondale Presidential Committee, the Reagan/Bush '84 Campaign, the Bush/Quayle '92 Campaign and the Clinton/Gore Campaign. The business conducted by the campaign organization is supervised by the White House, and the senior campaign staff are typically former White House staff members.

Developments which have reinforced the continued existence of the independent campaign committee include the Federal Election

Campaign Act of 1974, advancements in telecommunications and the expansive role of the media. Compliance with FEC law and the technological developments in communications require substantial staff expertise and management—responsibilities now fulfilled by the campaign organization. This chapter discusses the functions of the campaign organization, its activities, participants and structure.

FUNCTIONS AND ACTIVITIES PERFORMED BY THE REELECTION CAMPAIGN ORGANIZATION

The tasks of the campaign organization are substantial. According to a White House staff memorandum during the Carter administration:

> Generally, the campaign committee must be responsible for media, overall strategy and resource allocation coordination (with the White House), a field organization (with regional political operation and desk system), polling, moving the candidate and surrogates (political advance and scheduling), plus necessary research, press, legal, accounting, and other related functions. The campaign committee should also have primary responsibility for voter contact and GOTV [get-out- the-vote] programs, although the costs and mechanics of this effort (e.g., list acquisition, phone bank and computer costs) may be shared with other entities.[2]

Modern presidential candidates rely on this organization to fulfill the myriad legal, administrative and strategic tasks necessary to wage a national campaign.

Incumbent vs. Nonincumbent Campaigns

While campaigns perform four basic functions: campaign operations, research, public relations and finance, it is important to distinguish between incumbent and nonincumbent presidential campaigns.[3] The functions and activities of an incumbent and nonincumbent campaign are by no means identical. "If an incumbent president is seeking a second term, this will have pervasive effects on the electioneering."[4] A candidate's status greatly affects the structure and nature of the campaign organization.

Perhaps the most salient difference affecting the president's reelection campaign is the electoral advantage conferred to incumbent presidential candidates.[5] Just as there is an incumbent advantage in congressional elections, the president as candidate has substantial advantage over his challenger. Theodore White captured the essence of incumbency advantage when he wrote about the 1964 campaign:

> Lyndon Johnson was the Presidential Presence—and no challenger, at any time, can even approach the immense advantage that goes with being President. For, besides the majesty of the office, which cows the most hostile citizens to respect and attention, there are the facilities and the command that only a President can enjoy.[6]

As White's passage conveys, the president's most noteworthy advantage is his status. The presidential aura is a powerful resource.

In addition, the president has wide name recognition and his easy access to the media can be used to reinforce and expand this name recognition. "Everything the president does is news and is widely reported in all the media of information."[7] The president can focus on certain issues and draw public attention to them thereby forcing his opponent to react and respond. "As a general rule, the incumbent's advantage in an election is, in part, the advantage of being the leader to whom the challenger must react."[8] Further, the president can travel extensively at home and abroad in what are supposedly official business trips. Such travel and circulation among the electorate in his presidential capacity draw attention to the nation's leader and can enhance the prospects of reelection. Finally, the president's experience as chief executive is a substantial asset. Incumbents typically paint their opponent as inexperienced and thus unqualified for the prestigious position of what Thomas Cronin refers to as the "symbolic apex of the country."[9]

Though the advantages of incumbency are many, there are disadvantages as well.[10] One scholar appropriately describes incumbency as a "double-edged sword".[11] The state of the economy, a four-year record in office and uncontrollable external events (e.g., the Iran hostage crisis) are all potential points of vulnerability. The president's record in office is wide open to criticism—observers can criticize him for everything he has and has not done, for broken campaign promises and trouble abroad. And the phenomenon of retrospective voting—voting for or against a candidate based on his/her performance in the previous term—is thought to play a pivotal role in reelection campaigns.[12] Further, the distorted public expectations of the presidency make it nearly impossible for any president to satisfy the electorate. By today's standards, the president must be a "Superman," solving a wide range of problems and providing all things to all people. In the era of multi-billion-dollar budget deficits and mandatory cutbacks, this is clearly an impossible standard to meet.

There are other practical obstacles as well when a president is seeking reelection. According to one campaign insider, Bush/Quayle political director Mary Matalin:

> It costs a great deal more money when you're in office to drag the campaign and White House entourage from one place to another. Not only is security much tighter for a president than for his opponent, which inhibits "movement," you've got Secret Service agents in a constant state of high freak, preventing normal people, the ones who are going to vote you back in, from getting up close. Also it's more difficult to be an incumbent because you've still got to govern. One of President Bush's biggest, endless complaints was that, when we kept him on the road for three days at a time, he felt he was neglecting the reams of work on his desk.[13]

Despite the "double-edged sword" characteristic of incumbency, incumbent status fundamentally affects the type of campaign the president conducts. For instance, it affects the campaign's ability to raise money, resource allocation, staffing and the basic functions of the campaign organization. Strategy is determined with the aforementioned assets in mind, and the structure and organization of the reelection campaign is largely a function of the president's position as incumbent.

This can be seen by comparing the typical structure of an incumbent's reelection campaign to that of a challenger. The predominant difference between an incumbent and non-incumbent reelection campaign is the role of the White House in campaign decisionmaking. According to former White House Counselor to the President, Edwin Meese, "The White House dominates [campaign] decisionmaking."[14] In nonincumbent presidential campaigns, the decisionmaking authority is vested in the senior campaign management—the campaign organization is an autonomous body responsible only to those within the candidate's organization. The president's reelection campaign organization, however, is overshadowed by the White House. Though the president's reelection campaign organization has senior staff, its ultimate decisionmakers reside in the White House. As pointed out in Chapter Two, in almost every case, the president's chief of staff oversees campaign operations and, in conjunction with other senior aides, makes important strategic campaign decisions.

And because of this White House involvement, the incumbent campaign organization does not reflect a full-fledged campaign apparatus. For instance, security, scheduling, advance and speechwriting are all tasks that are handled by the White House thereby minimizing the reelection campaign's logistical involvement. It shares the same goal as any campaign—to get their candidate elected—but on a day-to-day basis, its actions are at times abbreviated and modified because of incumbent status. Given the unique position of the president and the White House involvement, the president's campaign operation can be characterized as a "hybrid" organization.

Further, some of the duties performed by the campaign are simplified because it is an incumbent campaign. For example, it is easier to raise money, "People prefer to give money to a man than to a vast organization. Especially they prefer to give to Presidents, who can do so much to reward the donor."[15] Similarly, recruiting volunteers to support the president's reelection campaign is a task made easier by the president's visibility and fame. In terms of staffing, the president's team can call on veterans from the previous campaign, although the White House itself tends to be the dominant source for staffing the senior level of the campaign organization. The campaign organization also benefits from remaining loyal White House staff who can provide substantive information to the campaign on short notice. An additional task, polling, is simplified because the president's pollster typically continues established polling operations and expands them to meet the needs of the campaign. Finally, there is a cadre of surrogate campaigners, namely the Cabinet, vice president and first lady, many of whom are able to reach out to key constituencies on behalf of the president. These influential campaigners can ease the president's campaign burden by traveling to many cities that have less strategic significance or that are geographically inconvenient. Everyone wants the president to visit their hometown and the plethora of surrogates enables the White House to respond favorably to a greater portion of the numerous invitations.

Despite such variation between incumbent and nonincumbent campaigns, all campaigns must accomplish the nuts-and-bolts tasks of presidential campaigning: fundraising, budgeting, meeting ballot access requirements, meeting primary filing deadlines, complying with federal election laws, organizing a fifty-state field organization, recruiting personnel, establishing a volunteer network, researching key campaign issues and the opposition's record and the scheduling of surrogate appearances. A memo from the Nixon administration indicates that as of April 6, 1971, nineteen months before the general election, Jeb Magruder assigned thirteen task force chairmen to cover different aspects of the campaign: Primaries and Field Organizations, Citizens Committee, Convention Logistics, Convention Strategy, Advertising (Direct Mail and Media), Polling (Computers, Research), Democratic and Republican Contenders, Spokesmen Resources, eighteen to twenty-year-old vote, the Black Vote, the Women's Vote, the Middle American and Ethnic Votes, and the Farm Vote.[16] This extensive development of what is essentially a nascent campaign organization demonstrates the breadth that a president's campaign organization typically must assume, despite the substantial support and direction provided by the White House.

In summary, the president's campaign organization, like the challenger's, is a vigorous operation which consists of many overworked and underpaid staff members whose duties are vast and essential. The incumbent campaign, however, does operate in a slightly abbreviated manner compared to nonincumbent campaigns because of the influential role of the White House. The advantages and resources conferred upon sitting presidents lighten the campaign's burden by simplifying tasks or transferring them to the White House. As a result, it is more precise to characterize the president's reelection effort as a hybrid campaign which is essentially a joint venture between the White House and the campaign organization.

The Campaign Structure

Initially, the reelection campaign organization is composed of a small group of participants, many of whom previously worked in the White House. Others come from the private sector offering "outside the beltway" advice. Over time, the campaign staff composed of White House insiders and private sector types expands to include an even larger number of supporters. Many of these participants campaigned for the president in the previous election and others are newcomers.

The structure of the organization varies from president to president, but there is usually a single person who is said to be the campaign manager in charge of the day-to-day oversight of the campaign. These campaign managers are typically White House politicos-turned-campaigners with a wealth of experience and expertise. Set out below is a list of campaign managers.

Eisenhower—Len Hall, Chair of the Republican Party

Johnson—Lawrence O'Brien and Kenneth O'Donnell, Kennedy operatives, 1964[17]

Nixon—John Mitchell, Attorney General (resigned), Clark MacGregor, White House Congressional Liaison

Ford—Bo Callaway, former Congressman (resigned), Rogers C.B. Morton, Secretary of Commerce (resigned), James Baker, Undersecretary of Commerce

Carter—Tim Kraft, Assistant to the President (resigned), Hamilton Jordan, Chief of Staff

Reagan—Ed Rollins, Assistant to the President for Political Affairs

Bush—Fred Malek, veteran of the Nixon and Ford administrations

Clinton—Peter S. Knight, a former top aide to Vice President Gore and Washington lawyer-lobbyist

In addition to the campaign manager, there is often a campaign chair who is largely a symbolic leader of the campaign.

Nixon—Francis L. Dale, publisher of the *Cincinnati Enquirer*

Carter—Robert S. Strauss, former Chair of the DNC

Reagan—Paul Laxalt, U.S. Senator

Bush—Robert Mosbacher, Secretary of Commerce, General Chair of the Bush/Quayle Campaign, Bob Teeter, Presidential Pollster, Chair and Chief Political Strategist[18]

Other senior positions typically include deputy campaign manager, finance chair, public relations director (often in charge of direct mail, advertising, press, media, polling, communications), research director, field coordinator, volunteer coordinator, special constituency interests liaison (e.g., Blacks, women, youth), issues and director of speechwriting.

Though the tasks of all incumbent campaigns are similar, the structure of the campaign organization varies. Just as there are various models of presidential staff organization—Pyramidal (a tight hierarchical staff structure with a single individual at the helm) or Spokes of the Wheel (no designated chief of staff, but multiple advisers with presidential access)—one can also utilize such models to describe presidential campaign organizations.[19] Typically the structure of the campaign mirrors the structure of the White House staff; if the president has a Spokes of the Wheel staff structure, then the campaign organization will reflect a similarly decentralized structure largely because of presidential style or sheer preference.

President Eisenhower's disdain for politics may have led to the formation of the 1956 centralized campaign operation that was run out of the Republican National Committee. By allowing a loyal entity outside the White House to manage the reelection campaign, Eisenhower was able to minimize the distraction imposed by the campaign. At the same time, his chief of staff, Sherman Adams, was able to report to him on the progress of the campaign. And, keeping in line with Eisenhower's "penchant for compartmentalizing leadership roles," the campaign structure with Len Hall at the helm resembled the hierarchical staff structure at the White House. [20]

Johnson's presidential campaign in 1964 was a decentralized operation that involved consultation with various groups of personal advisers, Kennedy holdovers and DNC staff. "The most graphic way to describe the campaign organization of Lyndon Johnson is to say that it was organized—like his White House—on a radial, not a Pyramidal, model." [21] The efforts of the various institutional participants—White House, campaign organization and party—were not neatly divided. Rather, there was an overlapping of efforts which resulted in the sharing of staff and resources. This decentralization created what, in effect, were several points of contact for the President, points which Johnson felt comfortable with because it enabled him to keep in touch with every facet of the organization. "Hence the President had not one but many direct contacts with what was going on at the Committee and with the operating aims of the developing campaign." [22] On occasion, Johnson's involvement went so far as to request more bumper stickers or billboards. [23] This radial-style campaign organization no doubt suited Johnson's style and desire for intense involvement and supervision. [24]

Nixon chose to run a reelection campaign that was hierarchical in structure and completely independent of the RNC. Like Eisenhower and Johnson, the structure of the campaign reflected his White House staff structure.

> The same desire for control and for circumventing the party was evident in Richard Nixon's reelection campaign in 1972 ...

> Completely separated from the national party, even in title, the Nixon
> Reelection Committee . . . raised its own money, conducted its own
> public relations (including polling and campaign advertising),
> scheduled its own events, and even had its own security division.[25]

According to Jeb Magruder, "There was never any thought that we
would run the campaign through the Republican National Committee
rather than set up our own Nixon organization."[26] Nixon preferred to
have contact with as few advisers as possible and managed to do so by
instructing his chief of staff to limit access.[27] With Nixon loyalist John
Mitchell as campaign manager and H.R. Haldeman in command of the
White House staff, Nixon was able to receive focused reports on
campaign developments. Some speculate that Nixon's detachment from
the RNC, and thus a highly personalized campaign organization,
coupled with the extensive involvement of White House staff in the
campaign set the stage for the Watergate debacle. At a minimum, it is
interesting to note that the first time a president utilized an independent
campaign organization, it resulted in one of the biggest political
scandals in American political history.

While serving as vice president, Ford expressed the importance of
running the presidential campaign through the national committee.
However, after ascending to the presidency, President Ford altered his
strategy and established an independent campaign committee.[28] This
campaign organization was a decentralized, troubled organization that
experienced high turnover. "From the outset, the PFC [President Ford
Committee] experienced factional strife that was hardly mitigated by
the eventual resignation of two committee officers—treasurer David
Packard, a former Deputy Secretary of Defense, and campaign manager
Howard H. 'Bo' Callaway, who had served as Ford's Secretary of the
Army."[29] After the convention, the campaign was reorganized and
enlarged to include Reagan campaign staff and party professionals.
Though the organization was fraught with personnel upheaval, in
October it was characterized as having "pulled itself together for the
final thrust of the 1976 campaign."[30] And "pull itself together" it did as
witnessed by the extremely close election results in November of 1976.
Ford's desire to include the party professionals as well as Reagan staff

members resulted in a rather decentralized Spokes of the Wheel operation while at the time of the campaign, his White House staff reflected a Pyramidal structure.

The decentralized, troubled organization may have been the result of other factors. First, the inexperience associated with Ford's first presidential campaign may have affected the composition and dynamics of the campaign. Second, the brevity of Ford's tenure did not bestow all the advantages of incumbency upon him. Third, the desire to please all factions of the Republican party may have influenced him to expand his campaign staff to include the party and Reagan staff members, ultimately creating a fragmented organization. Finally, because Ford ascended to the presidency as a result of a series of bizarre events, not through the will of the people or the support of the party, his campaign faced unusual burdens (e.g. consolidating his own party) that other incumbent presidential campaigns have not faced or faced to a lesser degree.

Carter's 1980 reelection campaign was more centrally directed than Johnson's and Ford's, and participants were predominantly White House operatives. The campaign staff structure was hierarchical and consisted primarily of former White House staff members: Robert Strauss, Hamilton Jordan, Tim Kraft, Tim Finchem, Gerald Rafshoon, Tim Smith and Linda Peek, though a sprinkling of Democratic party operatives also managed to obtain senior positions.[31] Compared to President Johnson, the Carter organization was much more centralized. Rather than a radial staff structure complete with overlapping responsibilities and sharing of resources, the Carter campaign was centralized in a single body with the campaign manager at the helm, much like the chief of staff on his White House staff. Note that in the first half of Carter's term, no chief of staff per se existed. Over the course of his tenure, he appointed Hamilton Jordan as chief of staff (and eventually campaign manager) and reverted to the classic Pyramidal staff structure.

In the 1984 reelection campaign, Reagan named his long-time friend, Paul Laxalt, general chair of the RNC and campaign chair. Positioning Laxalt in the RNC was an attempt to demonstrate his interest in the RNC's role in the reelection campaign. In addition, Ed

Rollins, director of the Office of Political Affairs, was named campaign manager. Though the campaign organization was more influential than the party, the RNC and the campaign worked together to increase the number of registered Republicans and to "get out the vote." Unlike Nixon in 1972, Reagan sought to avoid the impression that the campaign was dominated by the White House and created a campaign organization which sought to incorporate the party.

Despite efforts to incorporate the party, the 1984 campaign was essentially a centralized structure run largely at the direction of James Baker, President Reagan's chief of staff. There were then essentially three leaders of the campaign: Paul Laxalt, Ed Rollins and James Baker, but Baker was most influential. Similarly, President Reagan's White House staff structure during his first term was not the classic Pyramidal structure; rather, he appointed a "troika" to oversee and manage White House affairs (Baker, Meese and Deaver) just as he did for the reelection campaign. Nonetheless, the dominance of James Baker reflected a hierarchical, Pyramidal model.

The Bush administration is a bit of an anomaly when it comes to campaign structure and composition. Roughly thirteen months before the election, Bush named three Republican loyalists to run his campaign, Fred Malek, Bob Teeter and Robert Mosbacher. None of these men served in the Bush White House, though Bob Teeter had been the President's pollster, and Robert Mosbacher served as Secretary of Commerce. This initial appointment of a troika of campaign advisers paved the way for what can be characterized as a decentralized campaign organization. Interestingly, he appointed all three campaign leaders at the same time and gave them three different titles, but did not clarify who was at the helm. Observers speculated that Teeter was at the helm because he was closest to the President and perhaps the best strategist. Complicating matters further, James Baker, in August of 1992, moved from the State Department to the White House. According to many news accounts, *he* was running the president's campaign. Thus it appeared that there were four different people running the campaign. "The unusual step of putting three people in charge of a campaign was quickly questioned by some Republicans, who worried that a campaign operation with what amounts to four chiefs—including the chief of staff—would be unwieldy and slow-acting."[32] Eventually, Robert Mosbacher moved to the RNC to run the fundraising end of the campaign and Robert Teeter assumed the role as campaign chair.

Shortly after these appointments, the campaign was enlarged to include other White House and administration officials (e.g., James Baker, Secretary of State, J. Michael Farren, Commerce Undersecretary for International Trade and Gary L. Foster, White House Deputy Press Secretary). In addition, election-year staff shake-ups at the helm of the RNC and the Pat Buchanan primary challenge obfuscated the role of the party. Though the structure of the campaign resembled the Spokes of the Wheel model, President Bush's lagging status in the polls motivated many Republicans to become involved with the reelection campaign and this development essentially increased the number of "spokes" reporting to the President. These "salvaging efforts" from various Republicans no doubt disrupted the initially proposed troika structure of the campaign operation.

While some White House staff members criticized the ineptitude of the campaign organization, members of the reelection campaign complained about the disorganization within the White House under Chief of Staff Sam Skinner. "Mosbacher is not alone in complaining about the White House staff. Vice President Quayle is said by associates to be dissatisfied; senior campaign aides have openly criticized the operation, as have some Bush state chairmen."[33] The staff turnover and multiple avenues of advice from all parts of the Republican party created a decentralized campaign structure.

President Clinton's reelection campaign basically reflected his preference for a modified Spokes of the Wheel structure. While his early administration was marked by disarray, large, unwieldy meetings and presidential overexposure, Clinton moved aggressively to eliminate these problems by demoting his long-time friend, Mack McClarty and appointing then Budget Director, Leon Panetta as chief of staff. Mr. Panetta decreased access to the president while still preserving the president's opportunities for advice from multiple sources. Staff members such as George Stephanopoulos, Harold Ickes, Douglas Sosnick and outside consultant Richard Morris were key strategists in the reelection campaign and as the campaign moved into high gear, the points of access slightly increased. President Clinton's reelection campaign reflected neither the strict, hierarchical structure nor the Spokes of the Wheel. Since the points of presidential access were deliberately limited, a better way to characterize the campaign structure would be to refer to it as a modified Spokes of the Wheel organization.

Set out below is a chart which summarizes the structure of the presidential staff and campaign structures. Note that the White House staff structure listed reflects the structure that was in place at the time of the reelection campaign. Various presidents started their term with a particular structure and then changed it to suit their needs. Presidents Carter and Ford are examples of presidents who began with a Spokes of the Wheel structure and eventually adopted the Pyramidal structure.

President	Staff Structure	Campaign Structure
Eisenhower	Pyramidal	Pyramidal
Johnson	Spokes	Spokes
Nixon	Pyramidal	Pyramidal
Ford	Pyramidal	Spokes
Carter	Pyramidal	Pyramidal
Reagan	Troika	Troika/Pyramidal
Bush	Pyramidal	Troika/Spokes
Clinton	Modified Spokes	Modified Spokes

In all cases but Ford, Bush and, to a certain extent, Reagan, the structure of the campaign organization reflected the organization of the White House staff structure. Though it is difficult to know exactly why this is the case, one can confidently speculate that just as presidential style plays a role in determining White House staff structure, these same preferences play a role in determining the structure of the reelection campaign organization.

CONCLUSION

Perhaps the most notable aspect of the president's campaign organization is its lack of autonomy. While the campaign organization tends exclusively to the business of campaigning, it is always in the shadow of the White House. An observer of the 1984 campaign astutely commented, "The real campaign chief would be Baker and the real campaign headquarters would be his office in the White House."[34] Major elements of a campaign organization, like staffing and strategic planning, are under the purview of the White House. The White House dominates election planning and no matter what entity a president designates as his nominal campaign operation, the White House is the true campaign headquarters.

This is not to say that the campaign does not serve important functions, only that it is not a lone actor. This chapter points out the functions and vast activities performed by the campaign organization, its personnel and structure. The prominence of senior staff members in the campaign organization is but one signal of the operation's importance to the president. Reelection is clearly a presidential priority, and the campaign organization is the single entity designed with that as its sole objective. Given the recent trend of establishing an independent campaign organization and its perceived importance as well as federal laws affecting campaign practices, this component of the president's reelection campaign is here to stay. In fact, "Nothing in sight appears likely to lessen the impact of candidate organizations on presidential politics."[35] Despite its role in presidential campaigns, however, one cannot forget that the reelection campaign organization is analogous to a marionette whose moves are carefully controlled by White House operatives.

NOTES

1. Strategically speaking, it is important for the president to have his own reelection campaign organization. In the case of Nixon, he wanted to distance himself from the party so that he could portray an image as a president of all

people—Republicans and Democrats alike. Establishing an independent campaign organization facilitated this strategy.

2. Memorandum, *CONFIDENTIAL*, To: Hamilton Jordan and Bob Strauss, From: Tim Kraft, Subject: Coordination of General Election Planning, dated March 24, 1980, obtained at the Carter Library.

3. The four basic campaign functions are identified by John Kessel in his book, *Presidential Campaign Politics*, Homewood, IL: The Dorsey Press, 1988, p. 127.

4. Crittenden, p. 239.

5. See Nelson W. Polsby and Aaron Wildavsky, *Presidential Elections*, Chatham, NJ: Chatham House Publishers, (9th Ed.), 1996, pp. 69,77.

6. White, (1965), p. 354.

7. Ibid.

8. John Aldrich and Thomas Weko, "The Presidency and the Election Process," in Michael Nelson (ed.), *The Presidency and the Political System*, (2nd Ed.), Washington, D.C.: Congressional Quarterly, 1988, p. 256.

9. Cronin, p. 43.

10. For a detailed discussion of incumbency advantage and disadvantage, see: Cronin, pp. 43–46, Polsby and Wildavsky, (9th Ed.), p. 69; and Stephen Hess and Thomas E. Cronin, "The Incumbent As Candidate," *The Washington Post*, August 20, 1972, pp. C1, C5; Timothy B. Clark, "Carter Plays Santa Claus For His Reelection Campaign," *National Journal*, April 5, 1980, p. 548; Timothy B. Clark, "A Learning Experience," *National Journal*, April 12, 1980, p. 611 and finally, for a satirical essay about the president's exercise of patronage in an election year, see Russell Baker, "It's George S. Claus," *International Herald Tribune*, September 9, 1992, p. 20.

11. Cronin, p. 45.

12. See Morris P. Fiorina, *Retrospective Voting in American National Elections*, New Haven, CT: Yale University Press, 1981.

13. Matalin and Carville, p. 161.

14. Interview with Edwin Meese, May 27, 1992.

15. James MacGregor Burns, *Presidential Government*, Boston: Houghton Mifflin Company, 1966, p. 171.

16. Nixon Presidential Materials Project, Box 46 White House Special Files, White House Central Files, Subject Files: Confidential Files 1969–74, Folder [CF] PL [Political Affairs] 1/1/71–8/31/71, [1971–74], Memorandum for H.R. Haldeman, From Gordon Strachan, Subject: Citizens for the Reelection of the President, pp. 2–3.

17. In the case of Johnson's 1964 race, he was thought to be his own campaign manager because he played such an integral role in campaign planning. Besides the President himself, O'Brien and O'Donnell played the most visible roles.

18. In late August of 1992, after James Baker became chief of staff, Robert Mosbacher became chief fundraiser for the Republican National Committee and Robert Teeter became the campaign chairman. Interestingly Teeter's position as campaign chairman was not a symbolic one as Teeter was thought to be the most influential leader of the reelection campaign staff.

19. The author is aware of the shortcomings (e.g., too simplistic, inaccurate in some cases) of these models, but uses them for illustrative purposes since there are interesting parallels between the White House and reelection campaign staff organizations. Note that Stephen Wayne discusses the organization but uses the terms "centralized" and "decentralized" when referring to staff structures. Stephen J. Wayne, *The Road to the White House*, (4th Ed.), New York: St. Martin's Press, 1992, pp. 176–177.

20. Cotter and Hennessy, p. 86.

21. White, (1965), p. 348.

22. Lamb and Smith, p. 157.

23. White, (1965), pp. 350–351.

24. As previously stated in Chapter Two, Johnson never had a chief of staff. Rather, he surrounded himself with a cadre of loyal advisers without a clear ranking. The campaign structure, therefore, seems to have accorded with a general management style.

25. Wayne, p. 177.

26. Magruder, p. 155.

27. See ibid, p. 59. This Nixon preference is also revealed in other behavior. For example, "Cabinet members had to accept that they lacked access to the President and that their dealings would be with Haldeman and his various minions." Ibid, p. 102.

28. See Kessell, (1984), p. 568.

29. Alexander, (1979), p. 301.

30. Dom Bonafede, "A Glimmer of Hope Burns in the Heart of the PFC," *National Journal*, October 2, 1976, p. 1376.

31. See Larry Light, "Carter's Style of Campaigning Provides Tough Competition," *Congressional Quarterly Weekly Report*, September 13, 1980, p. 2705.

32. Ann Devroy, "Bush Lining Up Campaign Team," *The Washington Post*, December 5, 1991, P.A9.

33. Ann Devroy, "Mosbacher Said to Urge White House Shake-up," *The Washington Post*, May 30, 1992, p. A11.

34. Schieffer and Gates, p. 182.

35. Crittenden, p. 134.

CHAPTER 5

The National Party Organization and Campaign Planning

An additional participant in the campaign, the national party organization, is much less influential than the White House and the campaign organization, but nevertheless contributes to both short and long-term campaign planning. This chapter begins with an explanation of the relationship between the president and the national party organization, followed by an examination of the role of the party organization in campaign planning. This overview reveals the presidential campaign's influence over RNC and DNC operations: as election day draws near, the national party organization alters its focus according to the needs of the president's campaign.

PRESIDENT AS PARTY CHIEF[1]

To paraphrase Clinton Rossiter, "the president wears many hats," and one of these non-constitutional hats is that of party leader. As party leader he assumes the following duties:

> . . . [selects] the national chairman and other top party officials, reminds his partisans in Congress that the legislative record must be bright if victory is to crown their joint efforts, delivers 'fight talks' to the endless procession of professionals who call upon him, and,

through the careful distribution of loaves and fishes of federal patronage, keeps the party a going concern.[2]

Recent experience indicates, however, that fulfilling the role of party leader is not a top priority for the president: "The national committee has little to offer the president; it is just another supplicant for presidential favors."[3] Modern day presidential politics feature a party organization playing a marginal role in the electoral process and an overworked executive who sees little to gain from courting the party leadership.

A fair reading of political history since 1956 indicates that with few exceptions, presidents have shied away from their role as party leader or used the party primarily to enhance the administration's stature. President Eisenhower unwillingly accepted such a role: "A President like Eisenhower accepted his party leadership reluctantly, holding that the White House should be above party. . . . During his two terms, Eisenhower resolutely, but not always successfully, shied away from partisan political duty."[4] Lyndon Johnson was simply inattentive to the needs of the party organization. Some observers even characterized him as antagonistic to the interests of the party. President Nixon was also uninterested in the party organization. "He [Nixon] assembled a team of personal loyalists in the White House who demonstrated a low regard for the needs and interests of the party organization."[5] In a White House Memorandum, H.R. Haldeman wrote, in no uncertain terms, "The President will not do any Party functions in 1971."[6] President Carter was so uninterested in the party organization that he was formally denounced by the Democratic party for his neglect.[7] Demonstrating the antipathy between the White House and the party, one Carter White House staff member forthrightly described the DNC as the "in-laws" who[m] you are forced to tolerate, "a bunch of pesky people who early on were more of a nuisance."[8] These presidents were either uncommitted to their role as party leader, uncomfortable playing the role of party chief or a combination of both.[9]

Presidents Ford and Reagan were the only presidents in this study who embraced their role as party chief.[10] Gerald Ford actively promoted the Republican party and claimed that, as president, he had an obligation to strengthen the party organization. However, his brief tenure and accidental presidency make it difficult to compare him to other presidents. President Reagan's tenure represented a drastic change of course from the Carter days, for he was the only modern full-term Republican president to embrace wholeheartedly his position as party leader. "Reagan's record of party leadership may be regarded as among the most successful in the modern era. He was a committed partisan who established and maintained congenial relations with the congressional party and the party organization."[11] Clearly Reagan's relations with the party were extraordinary when compared to other modern presidents.

President Bush, a former party chair himself, initially demonstrated his commitment to the party organization by appointing a loyal campaign confidant, Lee Atwater, to the position of party chair. After this appointment, however, there was much upheaval at the RNC. Mr. Atwater died while serving the President and his successor, Clayton Yeutter, was not known to be a savvy campaign strategist or close confidant like Atwater. Chair Yeutter eventually moved to the White House to focus on domestic policy and a young Republican, Richard Bond, assumed the position as Chair of the Republican Party during the 1992 election year. This turnover is not necessarily a negative reflection on President Bush's leadership; however, his tenure in office was neither marked by the kind of neglect which characterized the Johnson, Nixon and Carter administrations nor the enthusiasm which characterized the Reagan administration.

The Clinton administration was marked by a similar ambivalence. While President Clinton participated in numerous fundraising events, his extensive reliance on the DNC for lobbying purposes during the first half of his administration drained the national committee of vital resources. Shortly upon entering office President Clinton called upon the DNC to engage in vigorous lobbying on behalf of his legislative agenda. The two largest legislative endeavors, the economic package and health care reform, tapped much of the DNC's financial and staff resources. With the razor-thin victory for the economic package and the failure of health care reform, the administration had expended much of its political capital and depleted much of the DNC's resources. Further, given labor's staunch opposition to NAFTA, there was no way that the DNC could promote the administration's next initiative. The White House then sought lobbying assistance from private business and the DNC shifted its focus to the forthcoming midterm elections. Such efforts were too little too late as evidenced by the devastating 1994 midterm losses that stunned the Democratic party.

Shortly thereafter, Chair David Wilhelm resigned under biting criticism that he neglected the interests of the party while catering to the Clinton White House. Subsequent to his departure, the Clinton White House called for a dual chairmanship with Senator Christopher Dodd as the party's national spokesperson and Donald Fowler as the day-to-day administrator. So while the Clinton administration may have given the DNC a more visible role in presidential policymaking, it was not beneficial to the overall health of the party. The White House essentially "Clintonized" the DNC to the detriment of other party needs and long-term interests.

Such behavior continued after the midterm upheaval, but in a different manner. After the legislative debacles, the DNC turned its efforts to fundraising and here again the White House applied pressure on the organization to raise extraordinary amounts of money. In turn, their record-setting fundraising placed the party in an extremely controversial position; in its zealous effort to raise record sums of money, some of it was donated illegally or obtained from dubious sources. Allegations were raised before election day, but the DNC did not return donations nor provide detailed responses until after the election. In December of 1996, the *New York Times* reported, "While party officials argue that only a tiny percentage of their donations have come under question, they have been forced to admit that they made a series of mistakes, beginning with a decision in 1994 to disband a unit that had previously screened contributions and contributors."[12] Meanwhile the Republican-controlled Congress planned a series of investigative hearings. So while the party organization was responsive to the White House, the Clinton experience reveals problems inherent in an overly responsive party organization, or perhaps, more precisely, an overly controlling White House.

Despite the lack of party involvement demonstrated by some administrations, presidents are nevertheless concerned about party relations and typically appoint someone on their staff to oversee the party organization. In the case of Eisenhower, Sherman Adams, Chief of Staff, accepted this role. After the 1964 election, Johnson appointed Marvin Watson as liaison to the DNC. "With these and other top party officials Watson helped to plan the agenda for party meetings and membership, fundraising, and voter registration drives."[13] Watson was formally the president's appointment scheduler, but spent substantial amounts of time troubleshooting on political matters. Nixon's political staff was larger. He appointed H.R. Haldeman to oversee the efforts of Harry Dent, Murray Chotiner and John Sears. Jimmy Carter looked to his Chief of Staff, Hamilton Jordan and Political Affairs director, Tim Kraft to supervise party efforts. In Reagan's first term, James Baker supervised the efforts of the Political Affairs director Lyn Nofziger and later Ed Rollins. During Bush's term, the Office of Political Affairs' directors James Wray, David Carney and Ron Kaufman supervised a staff assigned to oversee party relations. And in the Clinton administration, Rahm Emanuel, Joan Baggett and Douglas Sosnick kept tabs on the DNC. All of the aforementioned individuals essentially assumed the president's responsibilities as party chief.

The bottom line, however, is that the modern day party organization serves the president and is essentially a "political wing" of the White House. In a memo to President Carter, political strategist Pat Caddell indicated that, "It is clear that if the DNC is going to be 'Carterized' and made a political wing of the White House, that requires a chairman who is a loyalist, and essentially a Carter insider."[14] Caddell realized that the president's freedom to appoint the party chair essentially allowed the president to convert the party organization into a "political wing" of the White House.

Given this opportunity, it is not surprising that most presidents have replaced the sitting party chair within the first two years of their term. In the cases of Carter and Reagan, the public reason for replacing the chair was due to an unresponsiveness to the presidents' needs.[15] However, the likely reason is political, with a president preferring to appoint a campaign confidant who has demonstrated loyalty, or using the position as patronage and repaying a political debt. In the case of President Reagan's retirement and President Bush's succession into office, one can see that even when the same party remains the "party of the president," appointing a new party chair remains the norm. Once George Bush was inaugurated, he immediately sought to maximize the utility of the RNC by appointing a well-known political strategist, Lee Atwater, to replace sitting chair, Frank Fahrenkopf.

Some argue that the president's control over party staffing is self-serving and devoid of a sincere desire to strengthen the party organization. "When a president subordinates the national committee and its chairman to 'his people' at the party headquarters, he is serving his own interests, often to the detriment of his party's."[16] Regardless of whether one thinks such an exercise is self-serving, the fact of the matter is that the national party organization has become an entity that has lost its autonomy.

Besides the party losing its independence, some argue that the much more serious consequence of presidential staffing is the party's outright favoritism for the incumbent president when he faces a primary challenge. There is no rule that requires the party machinery to remain neutral when the president is faced with a primary challenge. Nor is there precedent for such objectivity in other elections. The RNC and DNC frequently show favor to congressional candidates competing in primaries. According to a one-time Democratic congressional candidate, Thomas Cronin, "The Democratic Congressional Campaign Committee said I was an attractive candidate; they encouraged me and said they were delighted I was running, but I didn't get anything. They had trouble raising money and concentrated on incumbents and open seats."[17] And party staff members see nothing wrong with the party choosing sides, especially when there is limited funding for congressional races.

Nonetheless, presidential candidates challenging the incumbent decry the party for its unfairness. These challengers are quick to argue that the party should remain impartial until after the nominating convention. For example, in 1980, the DNC was chastised by the Kennedy camp for showing overt partiality for President Carter.[18] According to a former DNC staff member, Elaine Kamarck, "The

Kennedy people were furious that the DNC was stacked against Kennedy."[19] DNC Chair John White apparently saw no impropriety in this; indeed he even told Kennedy that this would be his posture. Prior to Senator Edward Kennedy's declaration of candidacy, White told Kennedy that he would be loyal to President Carter, just as the DNC chair during his brother's administration would have been to President Kennedy. At the time, Senator Edward Kennedy replied that he expected the DNC Chair to be loyal to Carter and that he had no plans to run.[20] Subsequently, Kennedy's plans changed and he criticized the DNC for its partiality toward President Carter.

Similarly in 1992, the RNC was criticized by challenger Pat Buchanan who thought he was not receiving the same treatment as President Bush. Buchanan's party problems were further exacerbated by the fact that he could not even get on the Republican ballot in some states. RNC Chair Richard Bond adopted a typical posture when, in a television news interview, he dismissed Buchanan's complaints without making any attempt to project an attitude of impartiality.

The party of the president is in a "Catch 22" situation; either it remains loyal to the president and risks public criticism for showing favoritism if there is a primary challenge, or it acts impartial and risks alienating the president, perhaps resulting in its playing an even smaller role in the reelection campaign.[21] In either case it has something to lose and in modern day elections it appears that parties have opted for loyalty to the president and endurance of the primary challenger's short-lived criticism.

Though many will argue, and perhaps rightly so, that the role of the national party should not include being the handmaiden of the president, it would be difficult to amend such customary behavior when presidential loyalists staff the national committee. Further, the party decides its own rules and it is unlikely that it would establish laws restricting its behavior by requiring impartiality. According to political parties scholar Leon Epstein:

> Indeed, national parties, though long visible through their conventions and national committees, remained almost entirely unknown in national law during virtually all of their history. Even

now they are not subject to anything like the regulatory control that is common for state parties under state laws.[22]

In short, challengers will continue to lodge futile complaints against the party for its partiality, rather than acknowledge this characteristic as an immutable one that they must confront upon challenging the president.

THE PARTY OF THE PRESIDENT: REELECTION CAMPAIGN FUNCTIONS

Unlike the president, who is often reluctant to play the role of party chief, the party organization enthusiastically accepts its role of assisting party members to win national office, particularly the presidency. In fact, Democrats established the first national party organization solely for coordinating arrangements for the presidential campaign.[23] Political scientist V.O. Key described this election-oriented role by stating, "The major objective of party organization is the winning of elections."[24] Though the president's personal staff and campaign organization have eclipsed the party organization in importance, the national committee still performs important functions designed to assist the incumbent president's campaign. These general functions include: fundraising, party-building and organizing the nominating convention.

Long-term Reelection Planning Activities

Though the official presidential campaign does not begin until the fourth year of a president's term, there are a number of long-term projects carried out by the party organizations. These activities can be divided into two groups; those that provide financial assistance to the president for political activities, either directly or indirectly, and those tasks that are nonfinancial "party-building" projects.

Financial Activities

Since the president's initial campaigning is wholly subsidized by the party, fundraising is an ongoing task at the national party headquarters. Typically, the national party begins the president's term by raising money to retire previous campaign debts and then raises money for future elections, particularly the presidential election. The party sponsors multiple fundraising events and direct mail drives throughout the president's term. The national party also sends mailings to voters in hopes of expanding its electoral base and financial support.

It is important to point out, however, that the environment for party participation in such reelection-related activity changed dramatically with the passage of the 1974 Federal Election Campaign Act. Former RNC Chair Frank Fahrenkopf described these laws as a series of "walls" which limit the party's ability to assist the president in his quest for reelection.[25] During an election year, the party can contribute a maximum of $5,000 to the president's primary campaign. Though the amount of money that can be legally contributed to the campaign itself is modest, the national committees can spend larger sums on party-building—organizing get-out-the-vote drives, sponsoring fundraisers, television advertisements, or voter-registration campaigns. The source of this money comes in the form of "soft money" contributions; instances in which businesses may contribute the maximum to the candidate and an unlimited amount to the party. The party, in turn, utilizes such money to assist the presidential candidate—thus enabling the initial contributor to circumvent federal election law. Such practices have become quite common and controversial and politicians frequently pledge, albeit half-heartedly, to close this loophole in campaign finance law.

According to federal election law, the White House cannot subsidize political activity at any point in the term so the party must report political expenditures made on behalf of the president. A memorandum from the Carter White House to the DNC indicates that the DNC must subsidize expenses that are political in nature:

You have asked whether the DNC should pay for ceremonial pens used by the President and for Pat Caddell's travel and related expenses when he comes to Washington to consult with the President or others at the White House . . . Since both types of expenses are political in nature, they should be paid for by the DNC.[26]

The party also subsidizes the president's early campaign trips to Des Moines, Iowa or Concord, New Hampshire.[27] Additionally, the party pays for such items as White House Christmas cards and presidential cufflinks given to devoted volunteers or contributors.

Compliance with FEC reporting requirements is a rigorous task that demands substantial staff effort and attention. Failure to comply can result in fines and possibly embarrassing, unwanted publicity. Nonetheless, the party's ability to provide financial assistance to the White House is extremely helpful because it cultivates political support for the long term and is vital in the earliest stages of the president's campaign when FEC law prohibits government subsidization of nonofficial business.

Often times, however, the distinction between "political" and "nonpolitical" expenses is blurry and may cause outsiders to question White House practices. In 1980, supporters of Senator Kennedy filed a suit against President Carter which sought injunctions against spending public money on salaries and travel expenses for federal officials on "essentially political trips." The Carter administration dismissed this effort as a political ploy and roughly one month later the judge dismissed the lawsuit citing weak legal arguments.[28] More recently, the Dole campaign wrote a letter to the FEC accusing the Clinton administration of using taxpayer's money to run the reelection campaign.[29]

The political/nonpolitical distinction is even more difficult to make in cases of presidential travel during an election year.[30] Is it a campaign visit or an official visit? How do you distinguish? In 1992, President Bush went to the home state of Democratic nominee, Bill Clinton, to present a prominent businessman, Bill Walton, with the Presidential Medal of Freedom. Typically the nation's highest civilian honor is given to the recipient in a quiet White House ceremony. Instead, the

White House staged a major public event in Arkansas. At this event, President Bush delivered a speech sprinkled with campaign rhetoric. The White House assured skeptics that the trip was "strictly nonpolitical." According to *The New York Times* report:

> Mr. Bush did plan this trip, which was made at taxpayers expense, largely by himself. He then ignored campaign advice that he would be hard-pressed to depict it as an official visit . . . By coming here, Mr. Bush was able to appear before a crowd guaranteed to give him a rousing welcome on a primary day in which the Bush campaign was hoping to deal a fatal blow to the candidacy of his Republican rival . . . [31]

To many observers, this did not look like a "strictly nonpolitical event." However, if the White House declares it nonpolitical, suspect impressions are ignored and taxpayers subsidize the travel. Some presidential travel is more overtly political. For example, trips to Little Rock on behalf of a member of Congress must be paid for by the party or the congressman's campaign.

Recently, this issue of presidential travel has become quite controversial. In March of 1992, the Subcommittee on Human Resources conducted a series of oversight hearings to study travel-related expenses of the President and White House personnel. The Chair of the Subcommittee, Paul E. Kanjorski, pointed out that the president is appropriated $100,000 for travel, though this amount would not come close to covering the frequent travel for the President and the White House staff. Thus the committee sought full disclosure of the President's travel—dates, places, purposes, staff in attendance, and the accomplishments of the travel. Interestingly, the White House members asked to testify refused to attend the hearings. In fact, at the first hearing all the witness chairs were empty. Subsequent hearings were canceled because of the White House staff's refusal to attend. A Subcommittee staff member, Mary Weaver, reported that in May, White House officials turned over some information which was simply unresponsive to the Subcommittee's inquiry. Interestingly, though Congress is required to disclose such information, the Judicial and

Executive branches are not, thereby discouraging the White House from revealing such information and leading to the White House perception that this investigation was a partisan attempt to deflect attention away from the "check-bouncing" scandal in the House of Representatives. White House staffers simply expressed their disapproval by not complying with the Subcommittee's requests.[32]

Nonfinancial Party Activities

There is a second group of party activities which are of an ongoing, nonfinancial nature—the strategic or partisan-oriented tasks. These include voter-registration drives, research, polling, grass-roots voter education efforts and the maintenance of communication channels between the national party organization and party officials, elected officials and other activists. In a memo to President Carter, Hamilton Jordan presented the White House perspective on the role of the party organization, "[Its tasks] include: stay in touch with Carter supporters, stay in touch with Democratic Party leaders and elites, help elect Democrats to Congress and governors' offices, monitor party rules for 1980, serve as information apparatus for the White House and support Administration objectives."[33]

One former DNC staff member during the Carter years recounted the establishment of the "Desk System;" a system in which party employees were responsible for maintaining contact with party members in certain regions of the country. In a sense, the system provided a point of contact for party officials, elected officials and constituents. This system was not designed solely for reelection purposes (in part, because it folded once the campaign committee was established), but to provide continuous information to party officials. By keeping in touch with various states, the DNC could monitor state party affairs as well as troubleshoot. Such an ongoing relationship also worked to foster a sense of loyalty between the president and the party leadership and provided information that was particularly beneficial when it came time to establish the president's campaign field operation or preliminary campaign strategy.

Under the leadership of Frank Fahrenkopf (1983–1988), the RNC had a similar regional desk system. The RNC appointed regional political directors who frequently visited and offered assistance to the state party offices and their activities. A regional finance director also assisted state and local parties in fundraising efforts. Once the campaign organization was established, the RNC offices would work with the regional coordinators in the campaign. Such a system produced short- and long-term benefits and enhanced the national party's relations with state and local Republican party organizations. And of course, to the degree that state and local leaders attributed such efforts to the sitting president or to "his people"—a common response—such efforts also worked to the president's personal electoral advantage.

Short-term Campaign Planning

Once the president's independent campaign organization is established, the focus and activities of the party organization change. There are three major tasks that the party takes on after the primaries: planning the nominating convention, fundraising (so that it can spend monies beyond the federal monies received by the nominee) and supplementing the efforts of the president's campaign organization. Perhaps the most salient feature of short-term planning is that once the campaign is in full swing, the party organization's major efforts are, in a sense, swallowed up or coopted by the campaign organization and a cadre of White House strategists. At this stage of the campaign, electoral and strategic decisions are made by close presidential advisers, the campaign committee assumes the bulk of fundraising responsibilities and the party is relegated to hosting the convention and supplementing designated campaign activities.

Convention Planning

One of the party's most important tasks in convention planning is the selection of a convention site. The party chair appoints a site selection committee composed of members from the national committee. Cities seeking visibility and perhaps a boost to the local economy submit proposals to the party site selection committee in hopes of hosting the convention. Members of this committee tour the prospective sites and evaluate the facilities. Among the site selection committee's considerations are facility availability, money, services, adequate security, political feasibility and geographical desirability during the summer. Perhaps the two most important factors are the availability of convention facilities and the amount of money and services the city has to offer. In the post-Watergate era, Congress decided to give the national committees a set amount of money to host the convention so that the parties could be less dependent on outside contributions. However, it is not at all clear that this federal contribution eliminated money as a major consideration: the site of the 1992 Republican convention (Houston) offered to contribute $10 million toward convention expenses.[34] Nevertheless, facilities and city services (e.g., security) continue to be top priorities for the site selection committee.

In addition to logistical details concerning the convention site, political considerations are also important. A state with a constituency that is known to be receptive to the party may be preferable to another state, or the president may feel indebted to a particular politician and request that the convention be held in his or her state. The committee typically rules out the likely nominees' home towns.[35] However, if an incumbent president has a preference, it is almost always favorably considered by the site selection committee. "For the party controlling the White House the personal preference of the incumbent president is usually the overriding factor in the final choice of the convention city."[36] Based on the experiences from Eisenhower to Bush, the president's preference tends to be the decisive factor in the site selection process.

In 1956, President Eisenhower exercised his prerogative by choosing the site of the Republican nominating convention, "But the issue [site selection] had been in effect settled early in 1955 when the President acceded to a proposal by Harry Collier, a California oil executive, to come to San Francisco."[37] In 1968, Lyndon Johnson accepted the invitation of Chicago Mayor Richard Daley after first declining the invitation of Philadelphia's Mayor James Tate on grounds that Philadelphia lacked sufficient hotel space. President Nixon requested San Diego as the convention site and the Republican site selection committee obediently fulfilled his request. In a strange turn of events, however, Nixon later changed his mind about San Diego and the site was moved to Miami Beach. "However, when word leaked out that a San Diego subsidiary of a multinational corporation, which had recently received a favorable antitrust ruling from the Nixon administration, had made a generous contribution to the Republican National Convention Fund, White House staffers 'persuaded' the Republican National Committee to make a last-minute shift to Miami Beach."[38] President Ford indicated a general preference for the Midwest and the site selection committee held the nominating convention in Kansas City. The Democratic convention site in 1980 represented a change from previous site selection processes. After various southern cities were ruled out because of their opposition to the Equal Rights Amendment, President Carter did not express a preference. Ultimately, the DNC site selection committee chose New York City. The 1984 convention site represented a return to presidential preference. President Reagan made an early commitment to the Governor of Texas to hold the convention in Dallas. "Presumably heavy Texas conservative support for Reagan at both the 1976 and 1980 GOP conclaves and the anticipated friendly galleries in Dallas were factors in the President's choice of that city."[39]

Breaking with tradition, the RNC selected Houston, George Bush's "official" residence, as the site of the 1992 Republican nominating convention. According to a party spokesman, "The President did not indicate a preference. The President wanted us to review all the sites carefully and select the best site for the convention."[40] The head of the site selection committee indicated that Houston was selected primarily because it was a "strong logistical and financial package."[41] Not only was the Houston site a break with tradition because it was the nominee's reputed hometown, but the site was supposedly selected without the president's recommendation. The Clinton administration opted for Chicago over San Antonio, New Orleans and New York City because of its prior support, strategic location and the DNC Chair's personal ties to the city. According to one source, "'Clinton did very well in the last election in Illinois and the Midwest. . . . And he must win the Midwest again. You have an incumbent president and it gets down to the politics of the presidency.'"[42] It is also the case that the

Chair of the DNC, David Wilhelm, had spent much of his adult life in Chicago and had managed the campaign for the sitting mayor, Richard Daley. These ties no doubt facilitated Chicago's selection as the host city for the 1996 Democratic convention.

Once the site is selected, planning the convention becomes a full-time job. Arrangements for transportation, security, lodging, credentials/tickets, network coverage, media facilities and convention proceedings are among the major tasks of convention planners. Advanced planning is critical given the extensive media coverage. "Blessed with a captive prime-time nationwide viewing audience that sometimes exceeds 90 million persons, party leaders soon decided to make the national conventions into grand productions."[43] The national committee expends vast resources preparing for the nominating convention—what they consider to be the party's quadrennial showcase appearance before the American people.

Fundraising

Though fundraising is a primary activity of any campaign, after the convention party fundraising assumes center stage because the last major infusion of money that the party can give to the president occurs at the beginning of the general election cycle. "The national committee of a political party may not make any expenditure in connection with the general election campaign of any candidate for President of the United States who is affiliated with such party which exceeds an amount equal to 2 cents multiplied by the voting age population of the United States."[44] In 1992, this amounted to roughly $10.3 million, according to an FEC staff assistant. This cap encourages the national party to work extremely hard so that they can raise and collect enough money to donate the maximum amount.[45]

Party Integration with the President's Campaign Organization

Another activity after the nomination is an integration of the efforts of the party organization with those of the president's campaign organization. The White House and campaign organization typically decide what role the party organization will play in the general election and how their resources can best be utilized. Illustrating the importance of integrating the party efforts with the Carter reelection campaign, Hamilton Jordan, in April 1980, suggested that, "We need to begin to develop a technical base now for coordinating activities within the party for the general election in a way that is compatible with the campaign and also supplemental to the campaign."[46] Often times, increased participation in "get-out-the-vote" drives and canvassing are party activities thought to be quite useful in the final hours of the campaign.

Though the party organization is integrated with the campaign during the general election period, its role is typically a marginal one. The reason for White House domination and relegation of the party organization is partly due to the fact that the president's ties to White House senior aides are much closer both literally and figuratively. An additional reason for the party's peripheral role is strategic. Sometimes presidents disassociate themselves from the party so that they can appeal to a broader audience or because their party is in the minority. For instance, Nixon's campaign strategy in 1972 was to present himself as above party—as a president eager to serve all Americans. In order to carry this off, the president deliberately distanced himself from the party organization. But while permitting the party only a peripheral role in campaign affairs, most presidents are still careful to exploit party resources once the campaign is in high gear. To maximize the utility of this entity, the president sends experienced White House staff members to the party organization to oversee the party's efforts. The Carter White House sought to staff the DNC with senior White House officials or well-known politicos in order to maximize the contribution of the party organization. In April of 1980, Hamilton Jordan wrote to the President,

> In this regard, we have recommended to John [White] that Chris Brown begin to plan and work on the DNC's general election program right away. Also, John has agreed that he needs a new, top-notch political director to manage the various political functions of the DNC. John White, Tim Kraft and I have talked about people like Jim Free and Les Francis.[47]

Chief of Staff Hamilton Jordan recommended two White House staff members (Free and Francis) and one campaign veteran (Brown) to manage general election planning at the DNC.

In the case of the Reagan reelection campaign, the White House sent Paul Laxalt to head up reelection campaign planning at the RNC. Senator Laxalt, a close friend of the President's, assumed the newly created position of general chair of the RNC in March of 1983. Rather than leave campaign planning in the hands of Chair Frank Fahrenkopf and other RNC staffers, the White House created a position for a well-known Reagan loyalist. Though it was clear that Laxalt was essentially laying the groundwork for the Reagan reelection committee and recruiting campaign staff, he publicly indicated, "My role is to coordinate the activities and keep the lines open between the party's different political entities—the RNC, the White House and the Senate and House campaign committees."[48] The national party has limited resources and multiple constituencies competing for them (e.g. congressional candidates, gubernatorial candidates, state and local party organizations). Given this scenario, it is not surprising that the president likes to "plant" a known quantity at the national committee to oversee campaign planning and to assure that the national committee gives the president's campaign the necessary amount of attention.

CONCLUSION

Certainly, the tide has turned from the days when the president was beholden to the party leadership to the days of White House domination of the national party organization. While this status is unlikely to change in the near future, it also seems clear that parties will continue to play a consistent role in presidential reelection campaigns. On this score, perhaps what is most interesting about the role of the party organization is the changing nature of its role. Though the role of party is secondary to the White House political operation at all times, the types of activities it performs on behalf of the president are directly related to the stage of the president's forthcoming campaign.

Shortly after the president is initially elected, the party organization engages in a variety of activities designed to facilitate the president's reelection: fundraising, research, polling, grass-roots efforts and attempts to foster relations with state and local party organizations. Once the reelection campaign begins in earnest and the president's campaign organization is established, such tasks become the domain of the campaign, not the party. As election day nears, the White House becomes more involved in reelection planning and its influence permeates the party organization even more. There are staff changes at the national committee which are the direct result of White House reelection planning. After the primaries, the party is a mere host of the convention and supplement to the campaign operation. Not only do the tasks of party organizations change as the campaign gets nearer, but the White House tightens the reins on this organization in order to maximize its utility in the general election campaign. This cycle of increasing White House control and decreasing party autonomy crosses party lines and reflects the vast influence of the president's reelection campaign on party operations.

NOTES

1. Portions of the argument in this section were previously published in the *American Review of Politics*. See Kathryn Dunn Tenpas, "Promoting President Clinton's Policy Agenda," Vol. 17, Fall 1996, pp. 283–298.

2. Clinton Rossiter, *The American Presidency*, Baltimore: Johns Hopkins University Press, 1984, p. 17.

3. Hess, 1988, p. 85.

4. Louis Koenig, *The Chief Executive*, New York: Harcourt, Brace, 1964, pp. 102 and 113.

5. Nelson, (1989), p. 632.

6. Memorandum for Dwight Chapin, From: H.R. Haldeman, November 30, 1970, obtained from the Nixon Project, Box 46 White House Special Files, White House Central Files, Subject Files: Confidential Files 1969–74, Folder [CF] PL [Political Affairs] 9/1/71–4/30/72 [1971–74].

7. See Rhodes Cook, "Carter and the Democrats: Benign Neglect?," *Congressional Quarterly Weekly Report*, January 14, 1978, p. 57. See also

Weko, pp. 85–86 for additional elaboration about tensions between the DNC
and the Carter White House, particularly in regard to the appointments process.

8. Off-the-record interview with former Carter staff member.

9. See Koenig, pp. 91–96. One source of tension between the president and
the party results from the composition of the president's electoral coalition. His
election victory is due to the support of Republicans, Democrats and
Independents. It is therefore difficult for the president to pay undivided
attention to his party without alienating a substantial portion of the electorate.
Another source of tension is the constitutional foundations of the U.S.
governmental structure which provide for "separate institutions sharing and
competing for power" (a phrase coined by Charles O. Jones). Given this
institutional setting, the relationship between the president and a congressional
majority from the same party is not always harmonious. There is no mechanism
which insures or fosters partisan cooperation and this creates a tense
relationship between the president and his party.

10. If President Kennedy had been able to run for reelection in 1964, he
would have been included in this list as well. The Kennedy family's close
association with the Democratic party fostered his partisanship and this link
presaged a strong party leadership role during his tenure. President Kennedy
speaking to the National Press Club about his conception of the presidency
declared, ". . . if he neglects the party machinery and avoids his party's
leadership—then he has not only weakened the political party . . . he has dealt a
blow to the democratic process itself." John D. Morris, "Kennedy Pledges Firm
Presidency," *The New York Times*, January 15, 1960, pp. 1, 14.

11. Nelson, (1989), p. 634.

12. Mitchell, December 27, 1996, p. A12.

13. Redford and McCulley, p. 176.

14. Patrick Caddell, "Initial Working Paper on Political Strategy,"
December 10, 1976, p. 28, obtained from the Carter Library.

15. See Taylor and Cannon, October 5, 1982, p. A5, and Hal Bruno,
"Democrats in Distress," *Newsweek*, December 19, 1982, pp. 25,28.

16. Robert Harmel, "President-Party Relations in the Modern Era: Past,
Problems, and Prognosis," in Harmel, p. 251.

17. Dom Bonafede, "Textbook Candidate," *National Journal*, December 18,
1982, p. 2172.

18. See Dom Bonafede, "Laxalt's RNC Follows a Simple Rule: A Minority
Must be Better Organized," *National Journal*, June 18, 1983, p. 1271.

19. Interview with Elaine Kamarck, July 24, 1991.

20. Interview with John White, August 13, 1991.

21. For an indepth discussion of DNC Chair David Wilhelm's problems with the Clinton administration, see Lloyd Grove, "Man on a Tightrope," *The Washington Post,* April 20, 1994, p. D10.

22. Epstein, p. 255.

23. See Crittenden, p. 128.

24. V.O. Key, *Politics, Parties, and Pressure Groups*, (5th Ed.), New York: Thomas Y. Crowell Company, 1964, pp. 315–316.

25. Interview with Frank Fahrenkopf, February 5, 1992.

26. Memorandum To: Paul Sullivan From: Doug Huron Re: Political Expenses, May 11, 1977, obtained from the Carter Library.

27. Note, however, that once the president has set up his own campaign committee, that committee pays for presidential campaign-related expenditures.

28. See "Political Notes," *Congressional Quarterly Weekly Report*, January 5, 1980, p. 34 and "Political Notes," February 23, 1980, p. 572.

29. Subsequently, the Dole campaign planned to file a formal complaint with the FEC. See "Dole Assets Clinton Broke Election Law, *The New York Times*, August 3, 1996, p. A8.

30. The FEC anticipated the difficulty and wrote detailed statutes, "(b)(1) For a trip which is entirely campaign-related, the total cost of the trip shall be a qualified campaign expense and a reportable expenditure. (2) For a trip which includes campaign-related and non-campaign related stops, that portion of the cost of the trip allocable to campaign activity shall be a qualified campaign expense and a reportable expenditure. Such portion shall be determined by calculating what the trip would have cost from the point of origin of the trip to the first campaign-related stop, back to the point of origin. If any campaign activity, other than incidental contacts is conducted at a stop, that stop shall be considered campaign-related." 11 CFR (1/1/91 Edition), Ch. 1, Section 9034.7, pp. 229.

31. Andrew Rosenthal, "Bush Visits Clinton Turf, Presidentially, of Course," *The New York Times*, March 18, 1992, p. A19.

32. See Bill McAllister, "Hill Panel Disputes Bush's Travel Costs," *The Washington Post*, July 22, 1992, p. A1.

33. Memorandum To: President Carter, From: Hamilton Jordan, Re: Ken Curtis Meeting, (no date), obtained from the Carter Library.

34. Martin Tolchin, "Republicans Select Houston for 1992 Convention," *The New York Times*, January 9, 1991, p. A15.

35. James W. Davis, *National Conventions in an Age of Party Reform*, Connecticut: Greenwood Press, 1983, p. 44.

36. Ibid, p. 47.

37. Thompson and Shattuck, p. 74.

38. Davis, p. 48.

39. Ibid.

40. Tolchin, January 9, 1991, p. A15.

41. Ibid.

42. Hanke Gratteau, "Luring Democrats No Easy Feat," *Chicago Tribune*, August 7, 1994, p. 1.

43. Davis, p. 45.

44. See *2 U.S.C. 441 (a)(d)(2)*.

45. Party assistance in fundraising during the final stages of the campaign is also helpful because federal employees are restricted from making contributions to the president's reelection campaign. According to *18 U.S.C. Section 603*, it is a felony for federal employees to contribute money to their employer, in this case the president. Since obvious supporters of the president are not allowed to contribute to the campaign, the party steps in and raises substantial amounts of money from other sources. "Memorandum for the Heads of All Departments and Agencies," from C. Boyden Gray, Counsel to the President, November 15, 1991.

46. Memorandum for the President from Hamilton Jordan: Meeting with Chairman John White at 2:00 p. m. Today, April 14, 1980, obtained from the Carter Library.

47. Ibid.

48. Dom Bonafede, "Paul Laxalt: He's Laying the Groundwork for 1984," *National Journal*, June 18, 1983, p. 1272.

CHAPTER 6

Implications of a White House-Centered Reelection Campaign

"I will do what I have to do to be reelected."[1] While nobody but President Bush can explain exactly what he meant, this examination of presidential reelection campaigns from 1956–1996 brings us closer to understanding the dual role that presidents play when seeking reelection. Further, this overview of the combined efforts of the White House, campaign and party organization boldly illustrates the sheer magnitude of a reelection campaign. This knowledge adds a new dimension to studies on the presidency as it sheds light on how an external event, one that has become a staple of first-term presidencies, influences presidential behavior and White House operations.

This chapter examines the principal findings of this book and discusses their implications for governance. Findings can be organized into those that fit pre-established patterns of White House development and thereby confirm some of what we may already think about presidential campaigns, and those that raise important questions about the ability of presidents to truly fulfill their role as president while acting as a candidate campaigning for reelection. In addition, the role of president as candidate elicits a discussion of reform, namely, the single six-year term. If the reelection campaign distracts the president from the business of governing, what can be done?

THE CENTRALIZATION OF CAMPAIGN POLITICS IN THE WHITE HOUSE: PART OF A LARGER TREND

Since President Eisenhower's 1956 campaign, there has been a shift away from party-run reelection campaigns to White House–centered campaigns. Of course it is not surprising that the reelection campaigns of 1956 and 1992 are vastly different, but the change in terms of the locus of campaign activity is indeed significant. Students of the modern presidency have long been interested in the evolution of the White House Office—analyzing trends, monitoring its size and discussing the impact of various developments. Of late, scholars have tended to focus on the expansion of the White House staff and the increasing centralization of the policy process.

Rational Choice Theory

Perhaps the most significant theoretical contribution in this regard has come from Terry Moe who documents White House efforts to centralize and politicize the policymaking process.[2] By centralizing policy functions, the theory goes, presidents seize greater control over executive branch policymaking, thereby increasing the possibility that presidents can more easily exercise policy leadership. And, more recently, Thomas Weko examines the evolution of the executive appointments process from this theoretical perspective and concludes that ". . . rational choice accounts remain the most fruitful and promising way of theorizing about the presidency . . ."[3] Given the current status of presidential reelection campaigns, rational choice theorists would find successive presidents' centralization of this project (reelection) to be in line with their expectations. Due to the heightened uncertainty of renomination and reelection, presidents must internalize reelection-related expertise and control in order to maximize the prospects of reelection. But while modern presidents have acted according to rational choice accounts, it is not at all clear that such behavior is "rational" for the president. As this book conveys, the business of governing is set aside for the business of campaigning, essentially abbreviating the president's four-year term and stifling policy initiative. In addition, those presidents, like Ford, Carter and Bush, who radically restructured their presidential staff in preparation for the campaign were by no means better off for having done so. In fact, those who dramatically altered their staffs tended to lose reelection. So while a rational choice account may have accurately predicted the dominant White House role in the reelection campaign, it is not at all clear that this is the most "rational" approach to running an incumbent's reelection campaign.

It is more likely that a reversion to the unitary model of presidential campaigning (in which presidents delegate the bulk of campaign-related tasks to the party organization) might alter the priorities of governing and campaigning such that governing remains the central activity. If the president and White House staff divested themselves of campaign responsibilities, the four-year term may, in fact, prove to be fruitful throughout that time period. And, as a beneficial side-effect, expanding the party's participation may serve to revive the party's role in presidential electoral politics. Advocates of "stronger" parties would certainly endorse any such effort to empower the party system, just as critics of an overburdened, bloated presidency would like to see the president divest himself of additional nongovernmental tasks.

In short, one can move beyond the realm of policymaking to electoral politics and trace a trend similar to that identified by Terry Moe. Over time, politically relevant resources have come to be found in the confines of the White House (in specialized offices like Political Affairs, Public Liaison and Intergovernmental Affairs). There has been a concerted effort to internalize political resources whereby the White House staff has enabled and equipped itself to respond to various demands of the presidential campaign and key constituents (parties, business and other political actors).[4] In addition, the sheer expansion of White House staff in the latter half of the twentieth century has enabled the White House to assume more responsibility for the reelection campaign. The modern White House staff possesses the capacity and requisite expertise to oversee and partake in reelection-related activity. In sum, there have been two important developments contributing to a White House–dominated reelection campaign: the heightened specialization and centralization of political activity within the White House and the concomitant expansion of the White House staff. The former development would, of course, not be possible without the latter.

THE PARTY'S PERIPHERAL ROLE IN THE PRESIDENTIAL ELECTORAL PROCESS

Explanation of the presidential campaign from the White House perspective also confirms conventional wisdom about the role of the national party organization. The reforms of the nominating process, the expansive role of the media and the dominant role of the White House in the presidential campaign have pushed the party to the periphery of the electoral process. According to a Reagan and Bush White House staff member present for the 1984 and 1992 campaigns, "My take on parties in general is that they really do not serve a lot of purpose except for the mechanics of putting on a convention."[5] Such sentiment is commonplace among former White House staff members.

Due largely to electoral reforms in the late '60s and early '70s, the days of party control over bundles of convention delegates and party oversight of the president's campaign are gone. No longer is the national party the logical purveyor of electoral resources; instead, the White House has endowed itself with such resources and has effectively marginalized the role of the party in presidential electoral politics.[6] Many scholars have documented the decline of parties more generally, and this study supports this decline as it relates to the national party organization and presidential electoral politics.

IMPLICATIONS FOR GOVERNANCE: WHAT ARE THE LIMITS TO PRESIDENTIAL INVOLVEMENT? THE WHO, WHAT AND WHEN OF THE PRESIDENT'S CAMPAIGN

To date, there has been no systematic analysis of the president's reelection campaign. That is, while many assume that the president's campaign is a permanent organization or the exact replica of the challenger's, this book demonstrates that the president, by virtue of serving as president and candidate, conducts a fundamentally different campaign. It defines the boundaries within which the White House staff participate in the reelection campaign by answering questions pertaining to who is involved in the reelection campaign, when presidents begin preparing for this event and what they do to prepare for the forthcoming campaign.

Though we know that early campaign planning begins in the White House, no recurring pattern exists to identify precisely those staff members participating in such planning. While it is difficult to identify a specific White House office in which campaign planning begins, since President Carter, the Office of Political Affairs has been a common starting point. In addition, the chief of staff is always involved in campaign planning as well as senior staff members and select Cabinet members. As election day draws near, campaign involvement also includes lower-level staff members whose jobs become increasingly relevant to the campaign (press, public liaison, speechwriting), and many often leave their White House position to campaign full-time for the president.

Accepting the fact that campaign planning does not begin on Inauguration Day and continue for four years, one can identify concrete short- and long-term campaign planning activities that occur midway through the president's first term. Long-term campaign planning activities focus on the recruitment of a campaign staff (particularly at the senior level) and strategy formulation. Short-term campaign planning activities include fundraising, strategic analysis and criticism of the opposition's record as well as the White House record, consideration of future policy initiatives, polling analysis, theme development and the establishment of a White House liaison to coordinate activities with the campaign organization.

Rather than jump on the bandwagon and agree with the cynical, media-influenced impression that presidents begin campaigning for reelection as soon as they are inaugurated, this book provides a well researched response to the question of when presidents begin to prepare for the reelection campaign. Findings in this book refute those who claim that the president is engaged in a permanent campaign, as research indicates that most presidents begin gearing up for the reelection campaign after the midterm elections. And the formal establishment of the campaign, as mandated by FEC regulations, occurs roughly twelve months before election day. Thus extensive White House involvement in the campaign occurs just before the fourth year of the first term.

A NORMATIVE ASSESSMENT OF PRESIDENTS AS CANDIDATES

Many believe that Congress is inoperative because of its myopic focus on reelection. There is ample literature about members of Congress and how the quest for reelection affects their tenure in office. It is a widely accepted notion that members of the House spend the bulk of their two-year term preparing for the next election.[7] Although members of the Senate only stand for reelection every six years, they too spend a substantial amount of their term gearing up for reelection, in large part because of the extraordinary costs of waging a Senate campaign. If this is the case for Congress it seems logical to ask a similar question about the presidency, especially in light of the evidence in Chapter Three that indicates that policy innovation declines during the latter half of the president's first term.

This book indicates that the president possesses a massive organization capable of managing and tending to the campaign's details. While the president is likely to be involved in high-level strategy meetings, he is not bogged down with mundane campaign details. Members of Congress, on the other hand, do not possess such a vast organization and are therefore more involved with all aspects and details of the reelection campaign. Despite the variation in campaign management styles, the president is nevertheless distracted by the campaign and policy innovation takes a back seat to campaign business. During a campaign year, presidents tend to that government business that absolutely demands their attention (foreign policy), but spend much of their time tending to the business of the campaign.

Some observers of American politics suggest that something should be done to enable senators and representatives to spend less time campaigning and more time legislating. And efforts have been made to reform the campaign finance laws as a means of decreasing the amount of time candidates spend fundraising. But, what about the president? Perhaps it is advisable to begin by exploring why one might be in favor of enabling the president to run for reelection, rather than seeking outright reform of the institution.

Presidents as Candidates

Acknowledging that the presidential campaign diverts substantial attention from the business of governing, deciding whether this state of affairs is affirmatively "good" or "bad" for governance is debatable. On the positive side, campaign-influenced behavior may in fact strengthen the hand of the president. One benefit of the reelection campaign is the unity and discipline it imposes on the Cabinet. Because Cabinet secretaries are frequently asked to campaign on behalf of the president, they deliver a message that rarely strays from the White House line. Whether Cabinet secretaries like it or not, they tend to minimize their public objections to White House policy, thereby circulating the president's central message and demonstrating their support. Since Cabinet secretaries do not always reserve their criticism of the White House, a period in which such behavior is taboo can only benefit the president. Activities that increase presidential prestige, according to Richard Neustadt, facilitate governing from the president's perspective.[8]

Presidential reelection activity may also enhance certain aspects of governing. In an election year, presidents are compelled to focus on issues of great public concern.

> Spring of the election year is the season one hears politicians voicing unfamiliar concerns, in some instances the same concerns they had turned a deaf ear to only a few months earlier. Perhaps not coincidentally, presidents tend to become more popular during the six months preceding the beginning of the reelection campaign.[9]

Often the campaign rhetoric from the opposition party forces the president to respond, frequently to pressing domestic issues. President Bush, for example, refocused his attention from the "New World Order" to domestic concerns. And Bush has not been the only president to adapt his agenda to the reelection cycle. According to *The New York Times*, "President Nixon brought American troops home from Vietnam, slapped on wage and price controls, went to China and moved toward detente with the Russians, in each case reversing prior positions while bowing to public opinion."[10] The pressures of the campaign, especially the campaign rhetoric coming from the opposition party, no doubt motivate the president to address pressing issues—ones that were likely to have been neglected in the past.

An additional positive aspect of presidents seeking reelection is that it puts them back in touch with many of the citizens who elected them in the first place. The president, as candidate, is forced to leave the inside-the-beltway political cocoon to obtain a fresh, unvarnished perspective on problems facing the country. In an election year, it is not uncommon for the president to meet with constituency groups, many of whom feel that the president has neglected their issues and problems. President Reagan was well-known for his pre-election meetings with women, Hispanics, Blacks and veterans. Despite ulterior motives, it is nonetheless beneficial for the president to extend himself to these groups. Such meetings may encourage those disillusioned by politics and may prompt the president to act favorably on their behalf. Thus, the campaign imposes a sort of "reality check" on presidents and forces them to familiarize themselves with the citizenry, their grievances and opinions. According to Nixon Chief of Staff, H.R. Haldeman:

> In the fourth year, getting ready for the reelection campaign . . . is not totally a bad exercise in good government because what you are doing to be reelected may very well be what the electorate wants you to do as president. I don't think the responsiveness that is sharpened by the forthcoming campaign is necessarily a bad thing in government.[11]

The rallying around the president by Cabinet officials, the new-found attention paid to pressing issues and concerns, and the president's re-entrance into the public arena may serve to enhance governance as well as the president's prestige and strength.

On the other hand, electoral concerns can and do blur governing responsibilities, and this is problematic. According to Reagan staff member Lyn Nofziger:

> During the last two years, everything is really aimed at getting reelected. There is more of a focus on politics and less of a focus on principle. There is more of an emphasis on doing things that will help you win even if it's not good for your own policies.[12]

The preoccupation with politics over principle is probably not what the framers of the Constitution had in mind when they enabled presidents to seek reelection.

Certainly the business of governing does not come to a grinding halt nor does a crisis emanate from the distraction imposed by the campaign. Governing at the ground level chugs along oblivious to the campaign; for example, social security checks are sent to recipients on time. But, for a cadre of highly influential White House and executive branch officials, reelecting the president is the first and foremost concern and the dominance of politics over principle is the modus operandi. In effect, the reelection campaign whittles the four-year term down to a three-year window of opportunity for policy innovation. Presidents essentially have three years to enact their campaign promises; a period of time far too brief for any candidate to do so. The realities of campaigning are such that future presidential candidates would be wise to scale back their "I promise to do ___" list if they want to maintain some semblance of integrity. In an era of heightened presidential expectations, the reelection effort only exacerbates the problems that arise through the mismatch of inflated public expectations and presidential performance.

An additional charge against presidents seeking reelection is the use of government resources for personal gain. As Chapter Three explains, in a reelection year the president often, regardless of merit, strategically allocates grants to key primary states. Further, major policy reversals are made in order to appease a particular constituency. This practice enlarges the advantage gap between the incumbent and challenger and increases public cynicism by creating the impression that the president is essentially "buying votes." Presidents already enjoy a substantial advantage simply by virtue of their position so there is no need to permit them to stoop to the level of doling out patronage to strategic states and locales.

In an ideal world, presidents would be minimally distracted by reelection and all dispensation of government resources would be merit-based. The difficulty is that the public's notion of merit usually includes two conflicting requirements. We generally want presidents to demonstrate some ill-defined combination of responsiveness to public opinion and leadership without regard to such opinion. To help assure the former, we permit presidents to seek reelection; but in so doing, we pay the price of giving the president an incentive to adopt policies and behaviors that respond to public opinion, even in cases that may call for countermajoritarian leadership. It seems an insoluble dilemma, forcing us to choose between the current arrangement and one in which the incentives to respond to public opinion are reduced by prohibiting presidents from seeking reelection.

Perhaps the most commonly proposed reform designed to address the "problems" associated with presidents simultaneously managing the government and a campaign is the single six-year term initiative. Since 1787, roughly ninety proposals have been introduced with the hope of eliminating the demands and distractions of campaigning.[13]

The Debate

Proponents of this initiative argue that presidents seeking reelection take advantage of government resources to advance their political campaign. Such a state of affairs, they assert, damages the institution of the presidency. This complaint is one as old as the Republic itself. According to Alexis de Tocqueville:

> When a simple candidate seeks to rise by intrigue, his maneuvers
> must be limited to a very narrow sphere; but when the chief
> magistrate enters the lists, he borrows the strength of the government
> for his own purposes ... All public negotiations, as well as all laws,
> are to him nothing more than electioneering schemes. [14]

Such proponents claim that the office of the president loses its proper
constitutional function as it takes on a personal, "campaign" function.

Further, supporters argue that the campaign is an unnecessary
distraction. According to syndicated columnist Charles Bartlett, "I think
we have a president now who does not have a four-year term, but a
three-year term, because he is faced with the necessity of campaigning
in the final year of his term."[15] Presidents, as soon as they enter office,
are trying "to beat the clock" to get their programs enacted in time for
the forthcoming campaign. Realizing the importance of their record in
the forthcoming election, presidents seek solid achievements in order to
gain "bragging rights" in the reelection campaign. And, as many
presidents have learned, the constraints inherent in the legislative
process eliminate the possibility of quick results. Thus the need for
campaign preparation shortens an already brief period in which
presidents can propose and gain passage of their programs.

Other proponents argue that the current status of presidential
elections—its lengthy duration, expense and reliance on consultants—
has led to its departure from serving its proper functions, ". . . rather
than making the president independent of the legislature and
accountable to his constituents, it [the election] threatens to turn the
executive branch into a permanent campaign headquarters. . . . "[16] The
new business of campaigning in the television era is thought to require
even more time, effort and money than before, thereby infringing on the
president's time to an even greater degree.

But arguments to limit the president's tenure have not gone
unopposed. Those opposed to the single six-year term claim that the
prospects and politics of reelection heighten presidential accountability
and thereby serve the interests of a democracy. Jeane Kirkpatrick
argues, "I think, first, that to liberate presidents still further from the
temptations of ambition would, in fact, liberate presidents still further

from the discipline of accountability."[17] Kirkpatrick and other opponents of the single six-year term would prefer an executive who is distracted by the reelection campaign rather than a president who is essentially held unaccountable to the people for a six-year period.

An additional criticism of this reform is that it is antidemocratic in the sense that it fails to allow the citizenry to vote for a candidate whom they might like to see serve an additional term. By limiting the number of terms to one, it eliminates voters' ability to choose an experienced leader. Similarly, by limiting the president's tenure, observers argue that in the latter part of the term he will be a "lame duck," unable to govern effectively. In the words of Harry Truman, "You do not have to be very smart to know that an officeholder who is not eligible for reelection loses a lot of confidence."[18]

In the end, while both pro and con arguments for this reform are persuasive, the presence or absence of this reform will not eliminate current problems and may even create new ones. For instance, even if the single six-year term is adopted, presidents will likely campaign on behalf of their party. They may work to cast their administration in the best light so as to enhance the electoral prospects of their successor.[19] In the case of the Reagan administration's second term, they were extensively involved in efforts to assist the Bush/Quayle 1988 campaign:

> Throughout the fall campaign, President Reagan made good on his promises of support for the Bush campaign. Personal campaign involvement by the president included campaign appearances and money raising efforts for which he made himself readily available.[20]

In addition, the Reagan White House made itself useful in other ways:

> From key appointments to Presidential speeches, from legislative strategy to bureaucratic announcements, the Administration these days seems never to forget that there is an election coming . . . 'People across the Government are trying to be helpful to the Vice President,' a senior White House official said.[21]

Contrary to the hopes of single six-year term proponents, it is unlikely that adoption of this reform would eliminate presidential campaign activity and allow the business of government to enjoy the president's exclusive attention. Campaign and political concerns might intrude less, but they surely will not disappear.

A significant problem, mentioned by Jeane Kirkpatrick, which may arise with the passage of this reform is the decline in presidential accountability. Given a six-year ticket to govern, a chief executive can virtually chart a course without keeping attuned to the public pulse. In other words, a six-year term may be far too long for a "bad" president and too short for a "good" one. Perhaps in the latter years of the term, presidents may be more concerned with public opinion, but in the early years of the term there is little incentive to respond to public pressure. The absence of an electoral contest may produce unresponsive presidents who virtually ignore public sentiment. In short, adoption of the single six-year term will not solve the current problems associated with the reelection campaign and may even introduce new ones. Further, the unimpressive track record of the single six-year term initiative (ninety failed proposals) does not bode well for a likely amendment to the Constitution.

Despite the troubling side effects associated with presidents as candidates, the campaign provides a useful instrument of discipline in an administration, forcing the president to focus on issues of pressing public concern and prompting a critical evaluation of first-term performance. Perhaps it might be useful to expose a president's second term to similar pressures. Given this logic and the positive findings associated with presidents seeking reelection, it may well be prudent to repeal the Twenty-second Amendment, enabling presidents to run for reelection as often as they wish, rather than adopting reforms designed to eliminate presidential campaigning.

CONCLUSION

The emerging trends identified in this chapter bolster our understanding of presidents as candidates so that we can competently observe future presidents and decide to what degree their actions fit preestablished patterns. Observers of presidents in candidate mode should watch for increasingly politicized decision-making emanating from the White House, a more cohesive Cabinet, a president scaling back his policy agenda and reports of senior staff obsessed with campaign details. Furthermore, findings pertaining to presidents as candidates reveal the brevity inherent in the supposed four-year term and enable us to adjust our expectations accordingly.

The presidential reelection campaign has profound implications for governance: during a reelection year the business of governing is overshadowed by the business of campaigning. Such a state of affairs is not intractable, however, if presidents were more willing to rely on the party organization for electoral assistance. On the other hand, one should not underestimate the difficulty of reversing the enduring trend of increasing centralization and politicization within the institution of the presidency. Furthermore, the likelihood of convincing an administration to divest themselves of responsibilities, deemed by many to be the most critical of the first term, is not promising. One must make a strong case that minimizing the president's role as candidate would prove to be substantially more beneficial to both the administration and the country. At any rate, the sheer length of the American presidential campaign coupled with the vigorous participation of the sitting president creates a uniquely American phenomenon—one that deserves ongoing study and attention.

NOTES

1. Devroy, January 15, 1992.
2. Moe in Chubb and Peterson, pp. 235–271.
3. Weko, p. 155.
4. This phrase, "internalization of political resources," comes from an article by Richard Waterman in which he assesses the "expectation gap"—the difference between presidential resources/capacity and public expectations. See Waterman, pp. 23–29.
5. Background interview with former administration official.

6. Oversight of the party organization typically belongs to the White House Office of Political Affairs. For more information about this office, see Tenpas, "Institutionalized Politics".

7. See for example, Jones, 1967; Mayhew, 1974; Fenno, 1982; and Fiorina and Cain, 1987.

8. See Richard Neustadt, *Presidential Power and the Modern Presidents*, New York: Free Press, 1990.

9. Kernell, p. 187.

10. Tom Wicker, "Six Years for the President?," *The New York Times* (magazine), June 26, 1983, Sec.VI, p. 19.

11. Kernell and Popkin, p. 100.

12. Interview with Lyn Nofziger, May 5, 1992.

13. See *How Long Should They Serve*? American Enterprise Institute Forums: John Charles Daly, moderator, Charles Bartlett, Walter Berns, John C. Danforth and Jeane J. Kirkpatrick, American Enterprise Institute, Washington, D.C.: April 17, 1980, p. 1.

14. Alexis de Tocqueville, *Democracy in America*, (Vol. I), New York: Vintage Books, 1945, pp. 141–142.

15. *How Long Should They Serve?*, p. 4.

16. Bruce Buchanan, *The Citizen's Presidency*, Washington, D.C.: Congressional Quarterly, 1987, p. 191.

17. Ibid, p. 3.

18. Wicker, June 26, 1983, Sec.VI, p. 17.

19. See James Sundquist, *Constitutional Reform*, Washington, D.C.: The Brookings Institution, 1987, p. 45.

20. Harold F. Bass, "Comparing Presidential Party Leadership Transfers: Two Cases," *Presidential Studies Quarterly*, (Vol. XXIII), Number 1, Winter 1993, p. 123.

21. Steven V. Roberts, "White House Policy Makers Keep an Eye on the Election," *The New York Times*, October 5, 1988, p. A1.

Memorandum to the Next President Elected in the Year of the Millennium

What Works and What Doesn't in a Reelection Campaign

The 1996 election is over and pundits have offered their postmortems. Beyond the boredom and predictability of the '96 presidential campaign most everyone has their spin. There's no use crying over spilt milk or retelling the story of how your candidate could have won. Instead, let's look forward to the next president seeking reelection in the year 2004. By the time the president and his staff set their sights on reelection, they possess at least a twenty-four month record of achievements and mishaps. Nothing can change that, but presidents can improve their prospects of reelection through careful campaign planning and basic strategy.

These tips cannot revive a failed presidency, but can obviate criticism of a poorly run reelection campaign and the subsequent inference of a poorly managed White House. Campaign politics, of course, is far from predictable: a candidate can look untouchable one day and a month later be lambasted for possessing an inept campaign destined for failure. Candidates' stocks arbitrarily rise and fall. Given the volatility, control what you can—the composition of the reelection team, campaign strategy and organizational structure—and don't worry about the rest.

1. Don't delay planning.

First and foremost, begin preparing for the reelection campaign after the midterm elections: recruit veteran campaign organizers (experience matters), restructure your White House staff and get your fundraising mechanism in place. Don't be complacent because of high polling numbers, a legislative victory or uncertainty about seeking a second term. Rather than deciding whether to run, just assume you will and count on confronting a messy primary challenge. In other words, expect the worst. Remember, while ratings may be high in that third year, twelve to eighteen months is more than a lifetime in politics and a lot can change. Just ask George Bush.

2. Raise as much money as possible as early as possible.

Follow the Clinton model of raising money early. Not only did this deter potential primary opponents, but it frees the president from fundraising at a time when he should be trumpeting his achievements and outlining his plans for the future. In addition, money-grubbing during the campaign does little to enhance the presidential aura. Remember that anything that enhances the stature of the incumbent in the eyes of the public brings inestimable benefit to the campaign.

3. Look like a president.

Avoid overtly political events or posturing before the general election begins so that you can appear presidential and above the campaign fray. The worst thing to do is to forego the trappings of the office and stoop to the level of your opponent. Citizens are entranced and impressed by these trappings and, conversely, are annoyed by campaign politics. Adopt the Rose Garden strategy and hang on to it for as long as possible. Seek out patriotic events like the Olympics and wrap yourself in the flag—it's a winning strategy for an incumbent. President Clinton's avoidance of formally announcing his candidacy was a brilliant strategy. While many observers knew that he was in campaign mode, a formal announcement would have drawn even more attention to electorally-motivated decision making in the White House.

4. Don't hesitate, retaliate.

While maintaining the presidential aura, do not hesitate to respond to opposition barbs. Passivity is a bad thing. You do not want the opposition to have the last word, particularly when the story is negative—don't let it stick. Time is of the essence and any opportunity for a dip in the polls during the election year is potentially dangerous. You can bet that journalists will find hidden meaning in any drop in the polls and such news certainly makes for a great column regardless of whether the drop was meaningful.

5. Set the agenda.

The press and public already have a myopic focus on the presidency, so do what you can to control the news agenda. Be the newsmaker to the extent that there is positive news. Release negative news when there are bigger stories/events to divert attention. When there is negative news, try to distance yourself by using your staff as lightning rods to diffuse criticism. Whatever you do, don't let your opponent gain the upper hand in agenda-setting. You have the home-court advantage, so maximize it.

6. Follow the rules.

Adhere to the laws and ethical norms of separating campaign and government expenses. Make sure that your legal counsel impresses the importance of these guidelines upon all staff members. Your opponent will almost surely accuse you of using taxpayers' money to run the reelection campaign, so do what you can to guard against such criticism. Keep in mind that financial misconduct is a charge that citizens do not take lightly especially when it represents the misuse of taxpayers' hard-earned money.

7. Don't be the campaign tactician, at least not in public.

If you can, let your senior aides dictate campaign strategy (with your approval of course). If you can't keep your hands off, then keep your involvement in campaign strategy out of the public eye. Chances are that by the time the campaign is in high gear (January of the election year), you will be intimately involved in strategy meetings. To the extent possible, however, portray yourself as only marginally interested in campaign details. The citizenry want their president to fulfill the duties of the office, not spend the bulk of his time working toward self-preservation.

8. Take advantage of surrogate campaigners.

Let your popular Cabinet, family and staff members crisscross the country on your behalf. By virtue of their positions, they can appeal to select constituencies and bring great benefit to the campaign. In addition, they can enable you to focus your travel on only the most important locations and events.

9. The vision thing.

Make sure you have a theme or a solid program for your second term. Voters need a reason to renew your lease on the White House. So while it is important to proclaim your accomplishments, that alone is not a sufficient strategy. President Bush could not live solely off the Gulf War victory and his lack of an agenda for the future hampered his candidacy.

10. Be lucky.

Much of what happens in politics is luck—whether your candidacy is affected by uncontrollable events (e.g. the Iranian hostage crisis) or whether your opponent turns out to be a weak candidate (e.g. Goldwater). Recent presidents who have not secured a second term did not lose simply because of a failed presidency, but have been the unfortunate victims of circumstance: Ford confronted an abbreviated term, the Nixon pardon and was forced to govern in the aftermath of Watergate when voter cynicism was at a new-found height. Carter faced stagflation and the Iranian hostage crisis. Bush confronted a formidable third party challenge and an economy perceived to be in decline. Think positively and hope for the best. President Clinton perhaps best embodies the "be lucky" strategy. Despite a deluge of scandals, staff mishaps, legislative defeats and personal attacks which occurred throughout his first term, the "Comeback Kid" miraculously managed to rise above these sideshows and go on to victory.

Tips aside, the bottom line is that no matter how well you plan your reelection campaign, you could face the agony of defeat through no fault of your own. Nevertheless, it is preferable to be prepared; your reelection campaign efforts are a reflection of your presidency, staff and overall effectiveness. Not only that, but victorious presidents have all possessed a highly organized, efficient campaign operation. Learn a lesson from history. If you want to win (and who doesn't?), you need to invest the time it takes to establish a vigorous campaign operation.

Bibliography

Agranoff, Robert, *New Style in Election Campaigns*, Boston: Holbrook Press, 1976.

Alexander, Herbert E., *Financing the 1976 Election*, Washington, D.C.: Congressional Quarterly Press, 1979.

Alexander, Herbert E., *Financing the 1980 Election*, Lexington, Massachusetts: Lexington Books, 1983.

Alexander, Herbert E. and Monica Bauer, *Financing the 1988 Election*, Boulder: Westview Press, 1991.

Ambrose, Stephen E., *Eisenhower*, New York: Simon and Schuster, 1984.

Ambrose, Stephen E., *Nixon*, (Vol.2), New York: Simon and Schuster, 1989.

Anthony, Carl Sferrazza, *First Ladies*, New York: William Morrow and Company, 1991.

Asher, Herbert B., *Presidential Elections and American Politics*, (5th Ed.), Pacific Grove, California: Brooks/Cole, 1992.

Barber, James David, *The Presidential Character*, Englewood Cliffs, NJ: Prentice-Hall, 1977.

Blumenthal, Sidney, *The Permanent Campaign*, (Rev. Ed.), New York: Simon and Schuster, 1982.

P race, Paul and Barbara Hinckley, *Follow the Leader*, New York: Basic Books, 1992.

Buchanan, Bruce, *The Citizen's Presidency*, Washington, D.C.: Congressional Quarterly, 1987.

Burns, James MacGregor, *Presidential Government*, Boston: Houghton Mifflin Company, 1966.

Califano, Joseph A., *Governing America*, New York: Simon and Schuster, 1981.

Califano, Joseph A., *The Triumph and Tragedy of Lyndon Johnson*, New York: Simon & Schuster, 1991.

Cannon, Lou, *President Reagan: The Role of a Lifetime*, New York: Simon and Schuster, 1991.

Carter, Rosalynn, *The First Lady From Plains*, New York: Ballantine Books, 1984.

Casserly, John J., *The Ford White House*, Boulder: Colorado Associated University Press, 1977.

Ceaser, James W., *Presidential Selection: Theory and Development*, Princeton: Princeton University Press, 1979.

Childs, Marquis, *Eisenhower: Captive Hero*, New York: Harcourt Brace, 1958.

Chubb, John E. and Paul E. Peterson (eds.), *The New Direction in American Politics*, Washington, D.C.: The Brookings Institution, 1985.

Clifford, Clark with Richard Holbrooke, *Counsel to the President*, New York: Random House, 1991.

Cotter, Cornelius P. and Bernard C. Hennessy, *Politics Without Power*, New York: Atherton Press, 1964.

Cox, Gary W. and Samuel Kernell (eds.), *The Politics of Divided Government*, Boulder: Westview Press, 1991.

Crittenden, John A., *Parties and Elections in the United States*, Englewood Cliffs, NJ: Prentice- Hall, 1982.

Cronin, Thomas, *The State of the Presidency*, (2nd Ed.), Boston: Little, Brown and Co., 1980.

Crotty, William, *Party Reform*, New York: Longman, 1983.

David, Paul T., Ralph M. Goldman and Richard C. Bain, *The Politics of National Party Conventions*, (Rev. Ed.), New York: University Press of America, 1964.

Davis, James W., *National Conventions in an Age of Party Reform*, Westport, CT: Greenwood Press, 1983.

Deaver, Michael with Mickey Herskowitz, *Behind the Scenes*, New York: William Morrow, 1987.

Dent, Harry S., *The Prodigal South Returns to Power*, New York: John Wiley and Sons, 1978.

Donovan, Robert J., *Eisenhower*, New York: Harper and Brothers, 1956.

Drew, Elizabeth, *Portrait of an Election*, New York: Simon and Schuster, 1981.

Drew, Elizabeth, *On the Edge*, New York: Simon and Schuster, 1994.

Edsall, Thomas, *The New Politics of Inequality*, New York: Norton, 1984.

Edwards, George C., III, *The Public Presidency*, New York: St. Martin's Press, 1983.

Edwards, George C. and Stephen J. Wayne, *Presidential Leadership*, New York: St. Martin's Press, 1985.

Ehrlichman, John, *Witness to Power*, New York: Simon and Schuster, 1982.

Epstein, Leon D., *Political Parties in the American Mold*, Madison, WI: University of Wisconsin Press, 1986.

Evans, Rowland and Robert Novak, *Lyndon B. Johnson: The Exercise of Power*, New York: The New American Library, 1966.

Evans, Rowland and Robert Novak, *Nixon in the White House: The Frustration of Power*, New York: Random House, 1971.

Fenno, Richard, *The United States Senate*, Washington, D.C.: American Enterprise Institute for Public Policy Research, 1982.

Fiorina, Morris, *Retrospective Voting in American National Elections*, New Haven: Yale University Press, 1981.

Fiorina, Morris and Bruce E. Cain, *The Personal Vote*, Cambridge, MA: Harvard University Press, 1987.

Ford, Gerald R., *A Time To Heal*, New York: Harper and Row, 1979.

Germond, Jack W. and Jules Witcover, *Wake Us When It's Over*, New York: Macmillan, 1985.

Glad, Betty, *Jimmy Carter: In Search of the Great White House*, New York: W.W. Norton, 1980.

Goldman, Peter and Tony Fuller, *The Quest for the Presidency 1984*, New York: Bantam, 1985.

Goldman, Ralph M., *The National Party Chairmen and Committees*, New York: M.E. Sharpe, Inc., 1990.

Greenstein, Fred I., *The Hidden-Hand Presidency*, New York: Basic Books, 1982.

Grimes, Ann, *Running Mates*, New York: William Morrow and Company, 1990.

Gutin, Myra G., *The President's Partner*, New York: Greenwood Press, 1989.

Haldeman, H.R., *The Haldeman Diaries*, New York: Putnam, 1994.

Hargrove, Erwin C., *The Power of the Modern Presidency*, New York: Knopf, 1974.

Hargrove, Erwin C., *Presidential Leadership*, New York: Macmillan, 1966.

Harmel, Robert, *Presidents and Their Parties*, New York: Praeger, 1984.

Hart, John, *The Presidential Branch*, (2nd Ed.), Chatham, NJ: Chatham House Press, 1995.

Hartmann, Robert, *Palace Politics*, New York: McGraw-Hill, 1980.

Herrnson, Paul, *Party Campaigning in the 1980's*, Cambridge: Harvard University Press, 1988.

Hess, Stephen, *Organizing the Presidency*, (Rev. Ed.), Washington, D.C.: The Brookings Institution, 1988.

Hess, Stephen, *The Presidential Campaign*, (3rd Ed.), Washington, D.C.: The Brookings Institution, 1988.

Hess, Stephen and David S. Broder, *The Republican Establishment*, New York: Harper & Row, 1967.

Hult, Karen M. and Charles E. Walcott, *Governing the White House*, Lawrence, KS: University Press of Kansas, 1995.

Johnson, Lyndon Baines, *The Vantage Point*, New York: Holt, Rinehart and Winston, 1971.

Jones, Charles O., *Every Second Year*, Washington, D.C.: The Brookings Institution, 1966.

Jones, Charles O., *The Reagan Legacy*, Chatham, NJ: Chatham House Publishers, 1988.

Jones, Charles O., *The Trusteeship Presidency*, Baton Rouge, LA: Louisiana State University, 1988.

Jones, Charles O., *The Presidency in a Separated System*, Washington, D.C.: The Brookings Institution, 1994.

Kernell, Samuel, *Going Public*, Washington, D.C.: Congressional Quarterly, 1986.

Kernell, Samuel and Samuel L. Popkin (eds.), *Chief of Staff*, Berkeley: University of California Press, 1986.

Kessel, John H., *Presidential Parties*, Homewood, IL: The Dorsey Press, 1984.

Kessel, John H., *Presidential Campaign Politics*, (3rd Ed.), Homewood, IL: The Dorsey Press, 1988.

Key, V.O., *Politics, Parties and Pressure Groups*, (5th Ed.), New York: Thomas Crowell Company, 1964.

King, Gary and Lyn Ragsdale, *The Elusive Executive*, Washington, D.C.: Congressional Quarterly Press, 1988.

Koenig, Louis W., *The Chief Executive*, New York: Harcourt, Brace & World, Inc., 1964.

Lamb, Karl A. and Paul A. Smith, *Campaign Decision-Making*, Belmont, CA: Wadsworth Publishing Company, Inc., 1968.

Lammers, William W., "Presidential Attention-Focusing Activities," in Doris A. Graber (ed.), *The President and the American Public*, Philadelphia, PA: Institute for the Study of Human Issues, 1982.

Lichtman, Allan J. and Ken DeCell, *The 13 Keys to the Presidency*, Lanham: Madison Books, 1990.

Light, Paul C., *The President's Agenda*, Baltimore: Johns Hopkins University Press, 1991.

Magruder, Jeb Stuart, *An American Life*, New York: Atheneum, 1974.

Matalin, Mary and James Carville with Peter Knobler, *All's Fair*, New York: Random House, 1994.

May, Ernest R. and Janet Fraser, (eds.), *Campaign '72: The Managers Speak,* Cambridge: Harvard University Press, 1973.

Mayer, Jane and Doyle McManus, *Landslide*, Boston: Houghton Mifflin Company, 1988.

Mayhew, David, *The Electoral Connection*, New Haven: Yale University Press, 1974.

McPhearson, Harry, *A Political Education*, Boston: Little, Brown and Company, 1972.

Milkis, Sidney M., *The President and the Parties*, New York: Oxford University Press, 1993.

Miller, Merle, *Lyndon*, New York: G.P. Putnam's Sons, 1980.

Monroe, Kristen Renwick, *Presidential Popularity and the Economy*, New York: Praeger Press, 1984.

Moore, Jonathan, (ed.), *The Campaign for President: 1980 In Retrospect*, Cambridge, MA: Ballinger Publishing Company, 1981.

Moore, Jonathan, (ed.), *Campaign For President The Managers Look at '84*, Dover, MA: Auburn House Publishing Company, 1986.

Morgan, Ruth P., *The President and Civil Rights*, New York: St. Martin's Press, 1970.

Nelson, Michael (ed.), *Guide to the Presidency*, Washington, D.C.: Congressional Quarterly, 1989.

Nelson, Michael (ed.), *The Presidency and the Political System*, Washington, D.C.: Congressional Quarterly, 1988.

Neustadt, Richard, *Presidential Power: The Politics of Power*, New York: John Wiley, 1986.

Ogden, Daniel M.,Jr. and Arthur L. Peterson, *Electing the President: 1964*, San Francisco: Chandler Publishing Company, 1964.

Patterson, Bradley H., *The Ring of Power*, New York: Basic Books, 1988.

Patterson, Thomas, *Out of Order*, New York: Vintage, 1994.

Pfiffner, James P., *The Strategic Presidency*, Chicago: Dorsey Press, 1988.

Polsby, Nelson W. and Aaron Wildavsky, *Presidential Elections*, (5th Ed.), New York: Charles Scribner's Sons, 1980.

Polsby, Nelson W. and Aaron Wildavsky, *Presidential Elections*, (8th Ed.), New York: Free Press, 1992.

Polsby, Nelson W. and Aaron Wildavsky, *Presidential Elections*, (9th Ed.), Chatham, NJ: Chatham House Publishers, 1996.

Rabin, Jack and James S. Bowman (eds.), *Politics and Administration*, New York: Marcel Dekker, Inc., 1984.

Ranney, Austin, and Willmoore Kendall, *Democracy and the American Party System*, New York: Harcourt, Brace and Company, 1956.

Redford, Emmette S. and Richard T. McCulley, *White House Operations*, Austin: University of Texas Press, 1986.

Regan, Donald T., *For the Record*, New York: Harcourt Brace Jovanovich, 1988.

Roberts, Charles, *LBJ's Inner Circle*, New York: Delacorte Press, 1965.

Roseboom, Eugene, A *History of Presidential Elections*, London: The MacMillan Company, 1970.

Rosebush, James S., *First Lady, Public Wife*, New York: Madison Books, 1987.

Rossiter, Clinton, *The American Presidency*, Baltimore: Johns Hopkins University, 1984.

Royer, Charles T. (ed.), *Campaign for President: The Managers Look at '92*, Hollis, NH: Hollis Publishing Company, 1994.

Salmore, Barbara G. and Stephen A. Salmore, *Candidates, Parties and Campaigns*, (2nd Ed.), Washington, D.C.: Congressional Quarterly Press, 1989.

Schieffer, Bob and Gary Paul Gates, *The Acting President*, New York: E.P. Dutton, 1989.

Schlozman, Kay Lehman, (ed.), *Elections in America*, Boston: Allen & Unwin Inc., 1987.

Seligman, Lester G. and Cary R. Covington, *The Coalitional Presidency*, Chicago: The Dorsey Press, 1989.

Shull, Steven A., *Domestic Policy Formation*, Westport, CT: Greenwood Press, 1983.

Spitzer, Robert J., *The Presidential Veto*, Albany, NY: State University of New York Press, 1988.

Sundquist, James, *Constitutional Reform*, Washington, D.C.: The Brookings Institution, 1987.

The Ripon Society and Clifford W. Brown, Jr., *Jaws of Victory*, New York: Little, Brown, 1973.

Thompson, Charles A.H. and Frances M. Shattuck, *The 1956 Presidential Campaign*, Washington, D.C.: The Brookings Institution, 1960.

Thompson, Kenneth W. (ed.), *The Virginia Papers on the Presidency*, (Vol. 4), New York: University Press of America, 1979.

Thompson, Kenneth W. (ed.), *The Nixon Presidency*, New York: University Press of America, 1987.

Thompson, Kenneth W. (ed.), *The Ford Presidency*, New York: University Press of America, 1988.

Tocqueville, Alexis de, *Democracy in America*, (Vol. I.), New York: Vintage Books, 1945.

Troy, Gil, *See How They Ran*, New York: The Free Press, 1991.

Tufte, Edward R., *Political Control of the Economy*, Princeton: Princeton University Press, 1978.

Waterman, Richard W. (ed.), *The Presidency Reconsidered*, Itasca, IL: F.E. Peacock Publishers, 1993.

Watson, Ricahrd A., *Presidential Vetoes and Public Policy*, Lawrence, KS: University Press of Kansas, 1993.

Wattenberg, Martin P., "The Republican Presidential Advantage in the Age of Party Disunity," in Gary W. Cox and Samuel Kernell (eds.), *The Politics of Divided Government*, Boulder: Westview Press, 1991.

Wayne, Stephen J., *The Road to the White House*, (4th Ed.), New York: St. Martin's Press, 1992.

Weisbord, Marvin R., *Campaigning for President*, New York: Washington Square Press, 1966.

Weko, Thomas J., *The Politicizing Presidency*, Lawrence, KS: University Press of Kansas, 1995.

White, Theodore, *The Making of the President 1964*, New York: Atheneum Publishers, 1965.

White, Theodore, *The Making of the President 1968*, New York: Atheneum Publishers, 1969.

White, Theodore, *The Making of the President 1972*, New York: Atheneum Publishers, 1973.

Wildavsky, Aaron (ed.), *The Presidency*, Boston: Little, Brown, 1969.

Wildavsky, Aaron and Nelson W. Polsby, (eds.) *American Governmental Institutions*, Chicago: Rand McNally and Company, 1968.

Witcover, Jules, *Marathon: The Pursuit of the Presidency 1972–1976*, New York: The Viking Press, 1977.

List of Interviews
(As of September 1996)

Albers, Bill, Deputy Assistant to the President for Political Affairs, Carter administration

Allen, Richard V., Member of the Nixon administration and National Security Advisor in the Reagan administration, interviewed on two occasions

Baux, Laurie, Deputy Director of Personnel, Carter administration, interviewed on two occasions

Beckel, Robert, Office of Congressional Liaison, Carter administration, interviewed on two occasions

Berman, Michael, Legal Counsel and Deputy Chief of Staff to Vice President Mondale, Carter administration, interviewed on three occasions

*Bond, Richard, Chairman of the Republican National Committee, 1991–1992

Brady, Phillip, Assistant to the President and Staff Secretary, Bush administration

Broder, David, Reporter for *The Washington Post* who has covered presidential campaigns since 1960

Cable, Bill, Office of Congressional Liaison, Carter administration

Card, Andrew, Deputy Chief of Staff, Bush administration

*Cardozo, Michael, White House Counsel's Office, Carter administration, interviewed on two occasions

Carney, Dave, Director of Political Affairs, Bush administration and National Field Director Bush/Quayle Campaign

Carp, Bert, Deputy Director of Domestic Policy Staff, Carter administration

Casse, Dan, Deputy Director of Cabinet Affairs, Bush administration, interviewed on two occasions

*Christian, George, Press Secretary, Johnson administration

*Corrado, Anthony, Carter/Mondale '80

*Daniels, Mitchell, Assistant to the President for Political and Intergovernmental Affairs, Reagan administration

*Donatelli, Frank, Assistant to the President for Political and Intergovernmental Affairs, Reagan administration

Eidenberg, Eugene, Assistant Secretary for Intergovernmental Affairs, Carter administration

Fahrenkopf, Frank, Chairman of the Republican National Committee, 1983-1989, interviewed on two occasions

Fitzwater, Marlin, Director of Communications and Press Secretary, Bush administration

Francis, Les, Assistant to the Chief of Staff, Carter administration, interviewed on two occasions

Freiberg, Ronna, Office of Congressional Liaison, Carter administration

Goodwin, Thomas, White House Personnel Officer, Carter administration

Harper, Edward, Assistant to the President for Policy Development, Reagan administration

Hecht, Tim, Deputy Director for Political Affairs, Bush administration

Hess, Stephen, White House Speechwriter, Eisenhower administration; Deputy Assistant to the President for Urban Affairs, Nixon administration; Presidential appointments to UNESCO, Ford administration, Consultant on Reorganization of the Executive Office of the President, Carter administration, interviewed on two occasions

Hutcheson, Rick, Staff Secretary to the President, Carter administration

*Jones, Jim, Appointment Secretary, Johnson administration

*Jordan, Hamilton, Chief of Staff, Carter administration

Kamarck, Elaine, Democratic National Committee, Director of Midterm Elections, Director of Compliance Review Commission, 1977–1980

Kaufman, Ron, Director of Office of Political Affairs, 1991–1992, Bush administration

Kolb, Charles, Deputy Assistant to the President for Domestic Policy, Bush administration

*Kraft, Tim, Assistant to the President for Personnel and Political Coordination, Carter administration, interviewed on two occasions

Liebach, Dale, Assistant Press Secretary, Carter administration

*McCleary, Joel, Office of Personnel and Political Coordination, Carter administration

*McPherson, Harry, Special Counsel to the President, Johnson administration

Meese, Edwin, Counsellor to the President, Reagan administration

Moe, Richard, Chief of Staff to Vice President Mondale, Carter administration, interviewed on three occasions

Nofziger, Lyn, Office of Congressional Relations, Nixon administration; Office of Political Affairs, Reagan administration, interviewed on two occasions

Rafshoon, Gerald, Director of Communications, Carter administration

*Rehnquist, Janet, White House Counsel's Office, Bush administration

Rendon, John, Executive Director of the Democratic National Committee, 1978, Director of Scheduᴵ᾿ g and Advance, Carter/Mondale Presidential Committee, 1979–1980

Rubenstein, David, Deputy Assistant to the President for Domestic Policy, Carter administration

Shields, Carolyn, Executive Assistant to the Press Secretary, Carter administration

Smith, Alicia, Office of Personnel and Political Coordination, Carter administration

*Spencer, Stuart, Campaign Consultant to the Ford and Reagan Reelection Campaigns

Tate, Dan, Office of Congressional Relations, Carter administration

Tully, Paul, Political Director of the Democratic National Committee, 1990–1992, Consultant to the Carter White House and veteran of four Democratic Presidential Campaigns

Tutwiler, Margaret, Special Assistant to the President and Executive Assistant to the Chief of Staff, Reagan administration; Assistant Secretary for Public Affairs and Spokesman of the State Department, Bush administration

*Weaver, Mary, Professional staff member, Subcommittee on Human Resources, U.S. House of Representatives, interviewed on two occasions

Wexler, Anne, Senior Assistant to the President for Public Liaison, Carter administration

White, John, Chairman of the Democratic National Committee, 1978–1980
Yeutter, Clayton, Chairman of the Republican National Committee 1990–
1991, White House Director of Domestic Policy Staff, 1992

*Asterisk denotes phone interview. All others were personal interviews.

Index